Public Works

in the realm of art and infrastructure

Chaim Bezalel

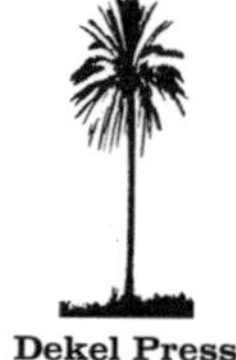

Dekel Press

ISBN: 978-0-9995958-2-4
Library of Congress: 2017962386

2nd Edition

To my wife, Yonnah, whose pioneering roots and buoyant spirit have motivated me, whose faith and pragmatism have sustained me, and whose love has brought me much joy.

Published by Dekel Press   www.dekelpress.com

Contents

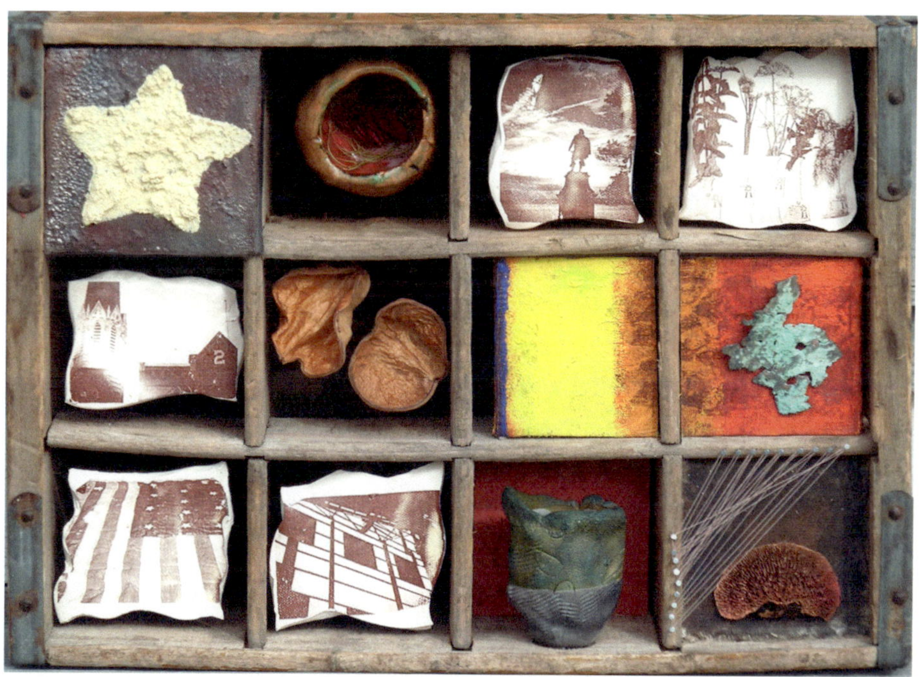

Stars and Stripes (2012) mixed-media in Canada Dry Crate, 12 x 19 x 6 in.

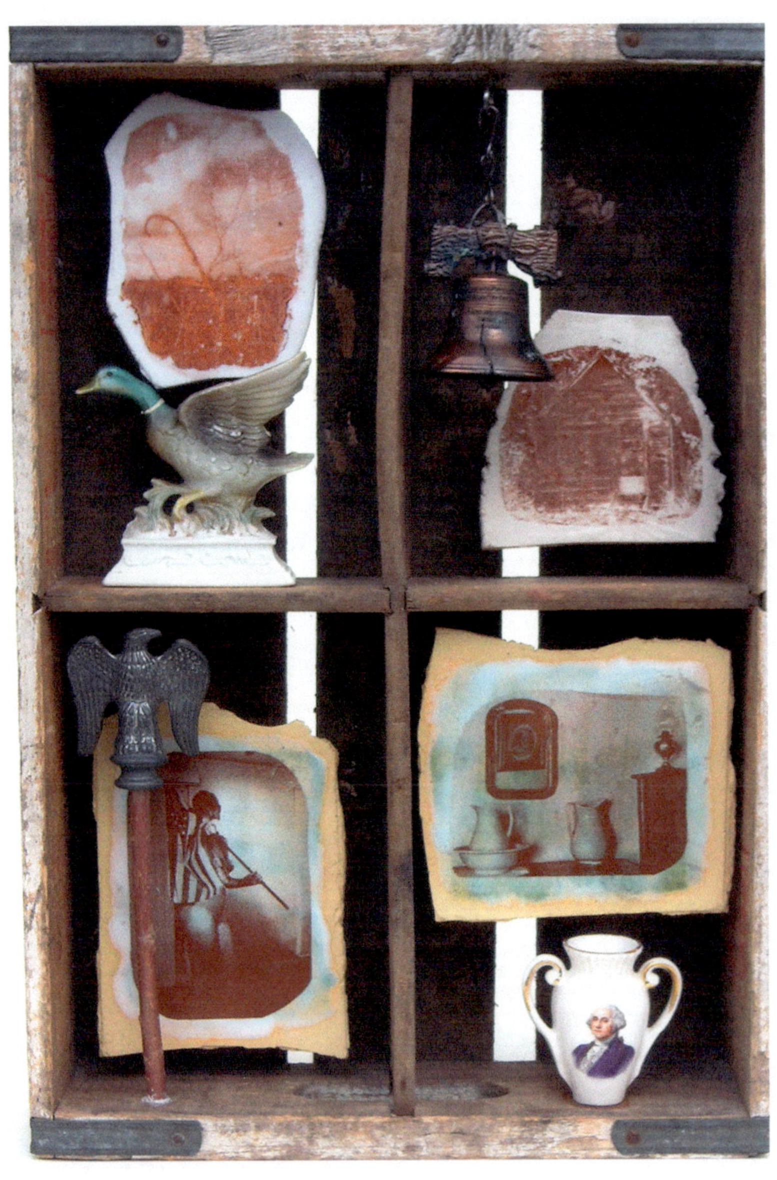

I WANT YOU (2007) mixed media in 7-UP crate, 19 x12 x 4 in.

Introduction

Wherever two or three are gathered, there ye shall have politics. Well, there were two, and we were laying in bed, my wife and I a few years back, listening to the morning news. And I was complaining every day until she couldn't stand anymore. She got even with me one day when she went to the city hall of Stanwood, Washington (population approximately 6,000 not including unincorporated areas). She had heard there was an opening for a seat on the planning commission, and also, she wanted to express her interest in the possibility of the city establishing a park on the bank of the Stillaguamish River, which borders the town. In any case, she landed up putting forward my name for the spot on the commission. Don't just lay there, in other words, do something!

And so I received an appointment from the mayor and joined the six other members. In the several years that I served I learned a few things. The first thing I learned was that I was not suited to the position. The meetings were long and for the most part boring. They dealt with picayune details on matters which I barely understood, not being a builder. In fact, I am severely handicapped in that I have no sense of direction. Furthermore the streets in this area are numbered according to a coordinate system. The numbers of the streets in this little town go higher than the streets of all of Manhattan and the Bronx. To be fair, they also start higher. So, in the meetings I spent a good deal of time lost. Nor am I a very good map reader.

I had recently begun wearing hearing aids, but even ramping up the volume did not allow me to hear the agenda as put forward by the Community Development Director, a very intelligent woman with a very dry sense of humor. She sat on the opposite side of the large fire department meeting hall from the dais where we commissioners sat. The reason for this choice of venue was to accommodate the public if it chose to attend, which was rare. We were all equipped with microphones, but the director, who spoke very quickly and almost sotto voce, never used hers. Thus, I began writing poems on whatever I was able to glean from the discussions. Some of them I read aloud during the meetings.

There was one aspect of the position for which I may not have been unsuited, though I felt otherwise. I am ambivalent about the entire idea of city planning. I realize that most laws are there to protect us from abuse of one kind or another. Though most people are not thieves, still we lock our doors at night. Building codes are necessary for safety and to protect the natural environment. On the other hand, modern urban planners, ever since Jane Addams established Hull House in Chicago in the late 1800's, understand that it is the unplanned and spontaneous interactions that create a living city. This goes beyond mixed use, or the mixing of commercial and residential in a neighborhood. The failure of the suburbs is in creating single use areas which exacerbated car culture, helicopter parenting and other ills. It is also the mixing of people from different backgrounds, cultures, and economic strata that creates a sense of excitement and participation, in short a community.

A high school friend, Blair Ruble, who has been working in a think tank in Washington DC, recently published a book, The Muse of Urban Delirium, which examines how new forms of performing arts emerge at moments of uncertain social identity in cities undergoing rapid transformation. The risk of over-planning is that it eliminates that necessary element of uncertainty.

I also learned that most people, at least at the lowest level of government are there with the hope of doing some good. We all know that the road to hell is paved with good intentions, but also, in spite of mistakes made with the best of intentions, people do learn from them. I sat with people who had been in this city all their lives and had served many years on the commission. The further back they went the more they remembered the presence of the river. I spoke with an old-timer who used to launch his fishing boat on the river and sail all the way to Alaska every year. I have also met more recent residents who were not even aware that there is a river.

The river was the reason why the town existed in the first place. The Stillaguamish River, like most of the rivers in the region, is named after the local Indian tribe. The very name Stillaguamish means people of the river. When whites settled the town in the 1870's, the first things they built were a steamboat dock and a sawmill. In 1943 a vegetable processing and refrigeration plant was built along 1500 feet of riverfront property. Since windows are undesirable in a refrigeration plant, the building resembles a prison. It was, however, the largest employer in the city for many years, and so, when it burned down in 1996, it was rebuilt in two months. Of course, like all forces of nature, the river has not always been benign. There is a photograph from 100 years ago in the historical society showing men in boats rowing down Market Street during the 100 year flood, a centennial event. While on the commission I advocated for access to the river, and was met with unanimous agreement. Since that time, the city has purchased an inactive farm right at the bend in the river, the most beautiful part, for a future park. It also purchased another parcel on the river where the lumber mill used to be. These two parcels are separated by the processing plant, which recently announced that it is moving its operations. The refrigeration plant will be sold or leased, but the building will probably remain. Redemption is a slow process.

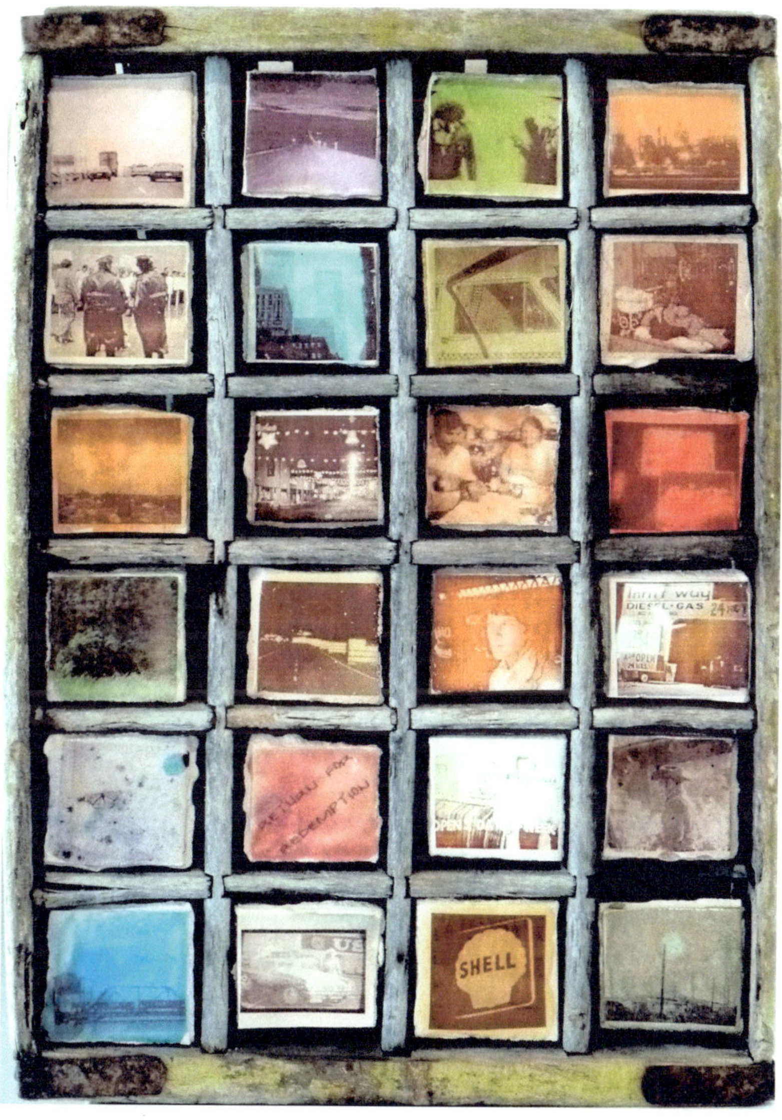

Return for Redemption (2011) ceramic tiles in Coca-Cola crate, 19 x 12 x 4 in.

Report from the Planning Commission

Twilight, Stillaguamish River

Still steely Stilly, silty slow riverrun
Like a serpent sloughing off its skin
Swapping courses slough and stream
Merrily life is but a dream.

Report from the Planning Commission #1

Banners and balloons are banned
Except if your opening is grand.
Flags are allowed
If the colors aren't loud

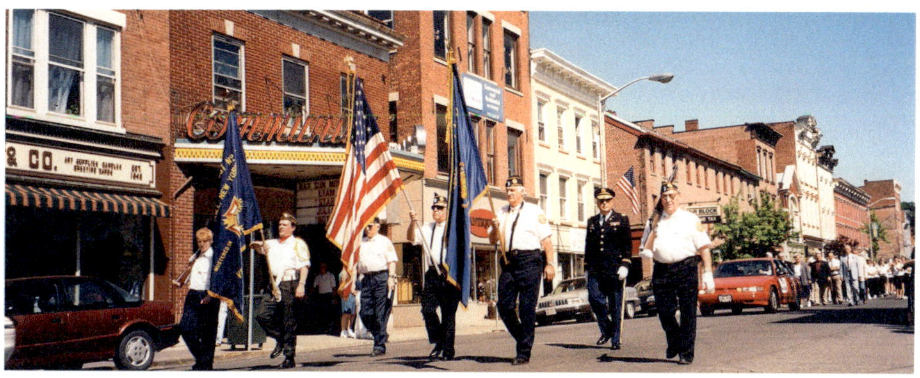

And they're followed by a full marching band.

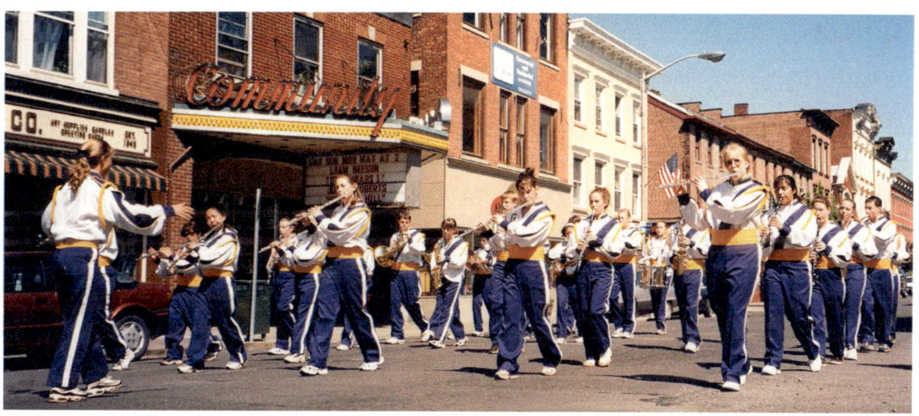

Memorial Day Parade, Catskill, NY (1998)

Report from the Planning Commission #2

Hold your invective
While we deliberate on collective
Gardens for cannabis.
Rein in your animus
It won't be grown near day care or schools
Abiding strictly according to rules.

We're discussing medicinal use.
It'll cure what ails ya, never fails ya,
And no one jails ya.
So now we have no excuse
Not to introduce
A zoned out zone where plants are grown
Maybe even fill the hole in the ozone.

Report from the Planning Commission #3

On chickens we're boosters
But restrictions on roosters.
Within the limits of the city
If you cackle and cluck
Or look like a duck
You're fair fowl, so resolved by committee.
But if you're free scratching
You'd better be hatching
Way out in some other zip code.
So take our suggestion
Or you'll answer the question:
"Why did the chicken cross the road?"
Each chicken coop
Must be kept clean of poop
Or else face removal or fine
And all of the pens
For these celibate hens
Kept five feet from the property line.

Report *to* the Commission

In England the mail's delivered
By appointment to the king.
In America we take a poll
To determine everything.

They had a revolution too
Except it didn't stick
Dismantling the palace of a duke
In Basing brick by brick.

Some of which were used in fact
To build the entire village
What now would be recycling
Back then was simply pillage.

A vast pasture fringed by trees -
The commons in Old Basing
Where horses can be kept for free
And cows in summer grazing.

We had our commons too Stateside
Except it didn't stick.
The name remains the very same
Developers often pick.*

**The Commons Shopping Center,*
   Hillsborough County, NH
The Commons At Sierrafield Development,
   Byron Center, MI
The Commons at Ballard, Seattle, WA
The Commons North Park, Midland, TX
Humboldt Commons, shopping mall, Humboldt, CA

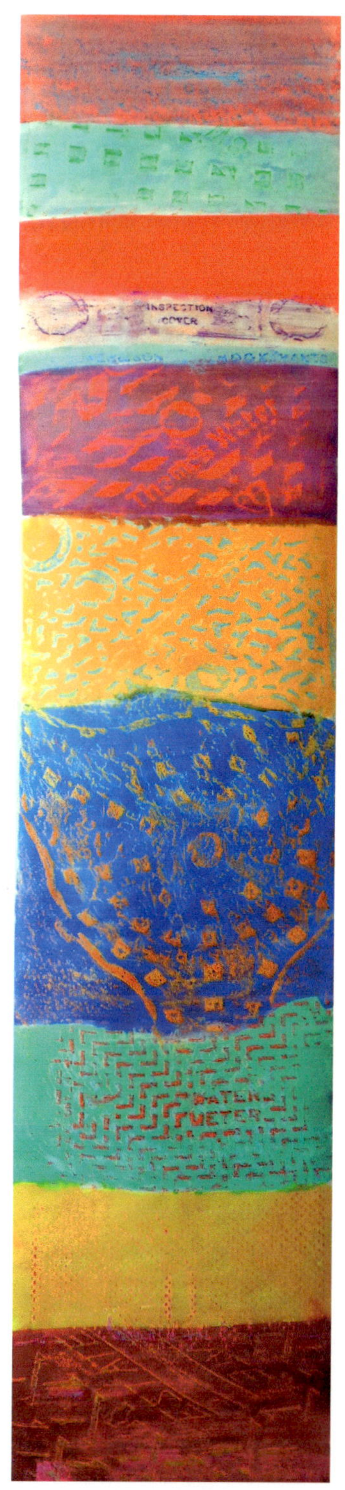

Thames Water (2014) Monoprint (crayon and ink)
from rubbings of utility covers in Basingstoke,England.
120 x 24 in.

Epilogue with Input from the City Council

There's many a slip twixt cup and lip
An old English proverb advises.
There may be a catch or there may be a blip
So don't count your chickens, life's full of surprises.

The Planning Commission recommended provision
For the sale of medicinal weed.
That zoning provision is in need of revision
Since pot became legal regardless of need.

Recreational, medicinal could be sold in one shop
With the latter exempted from tax.
So up went the shingle next door to the cops
So no one would think that enforcement was lax.

Two years later they changed their position
The deal thought done was not done.
"No prohibition if you've got a condition
But we don't want it used just for fun."

The public attended a subsequent forum
When the city council convened.
However the meeting was lacking a quorum
So the pot shop was still quarantined.

In the end they cut the Gordian knot.
Let the Feds be the Feds, and the states blues or reds
Decide for themselves the legality of pot
No sales in this city, not for meds or potheads.

Roads, Water,
Sewer, Gas, and Light

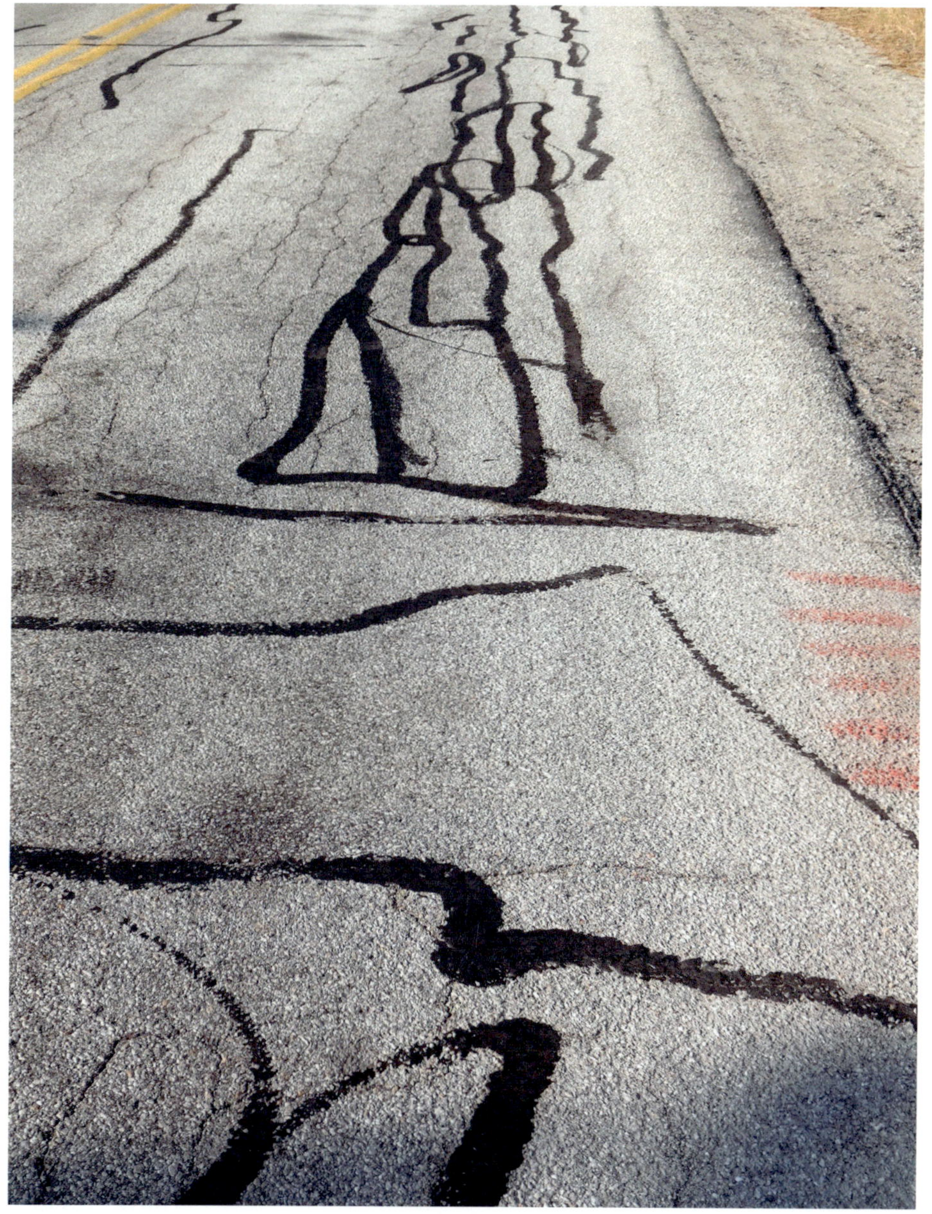

River Road, Plain, WA

Roadwork I (2014) 30 x 22 in. monoprint with printers relief ink and tar

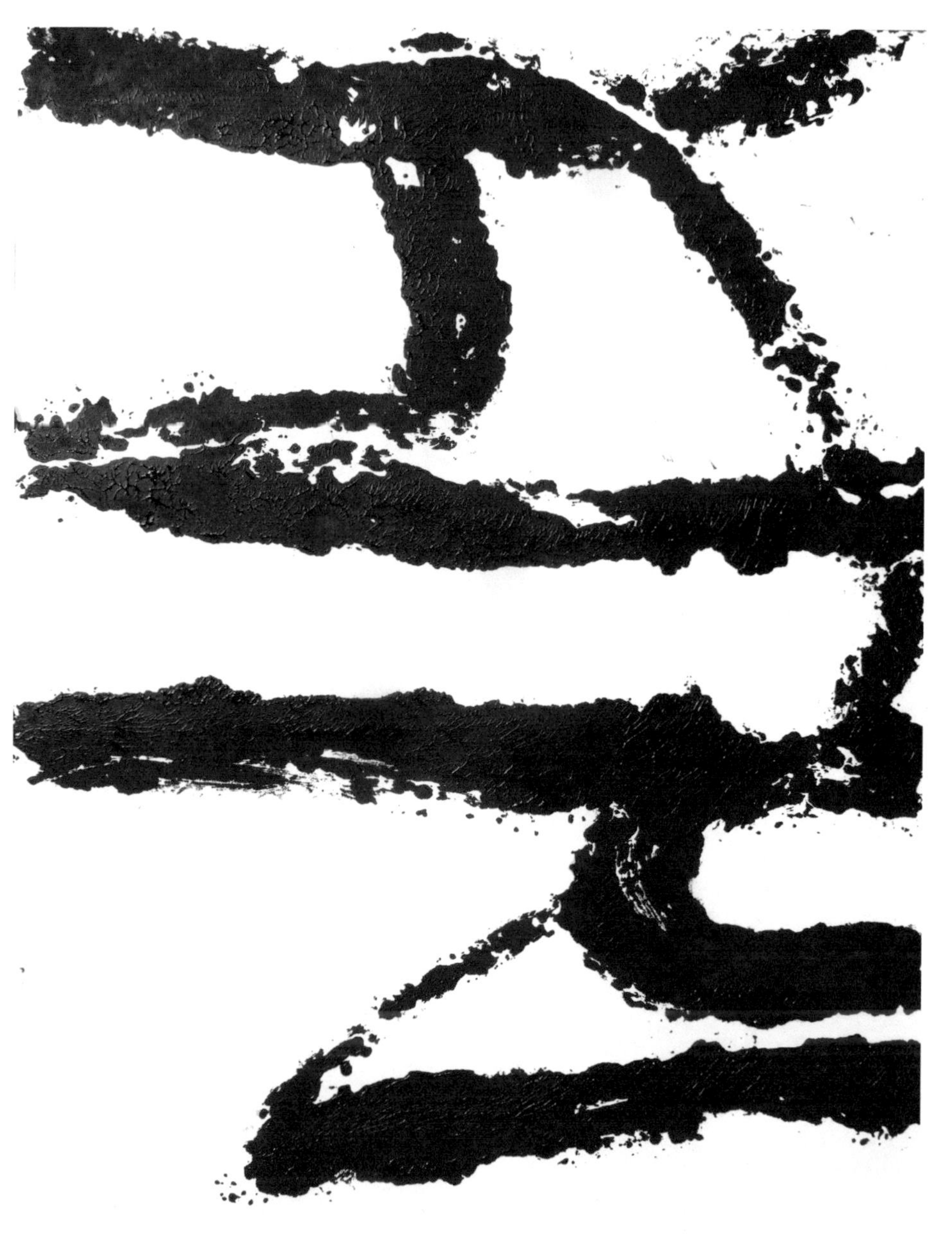

Roadwork II (2014) 30 x 22 in. monoprint with printers relief ink and tar

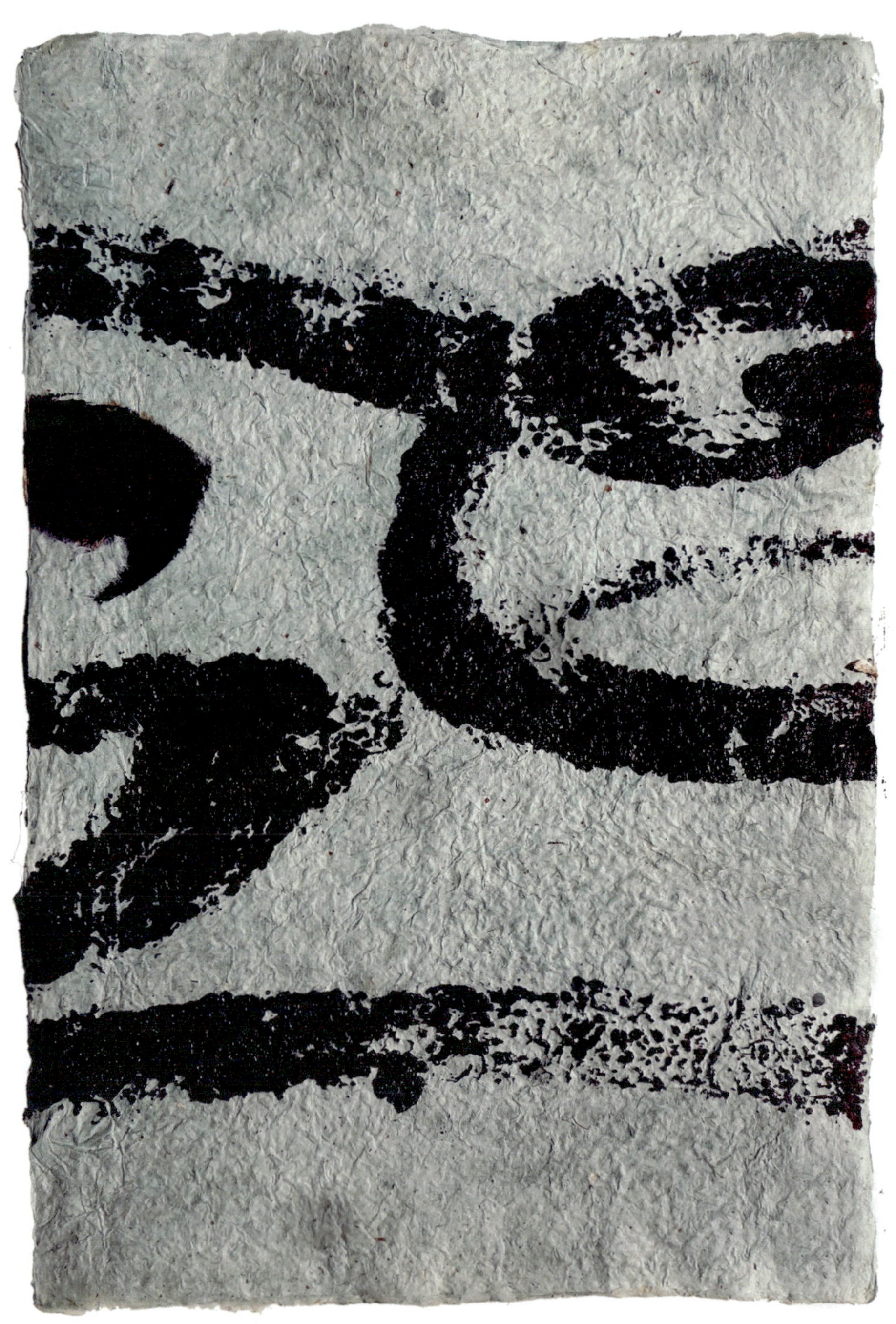

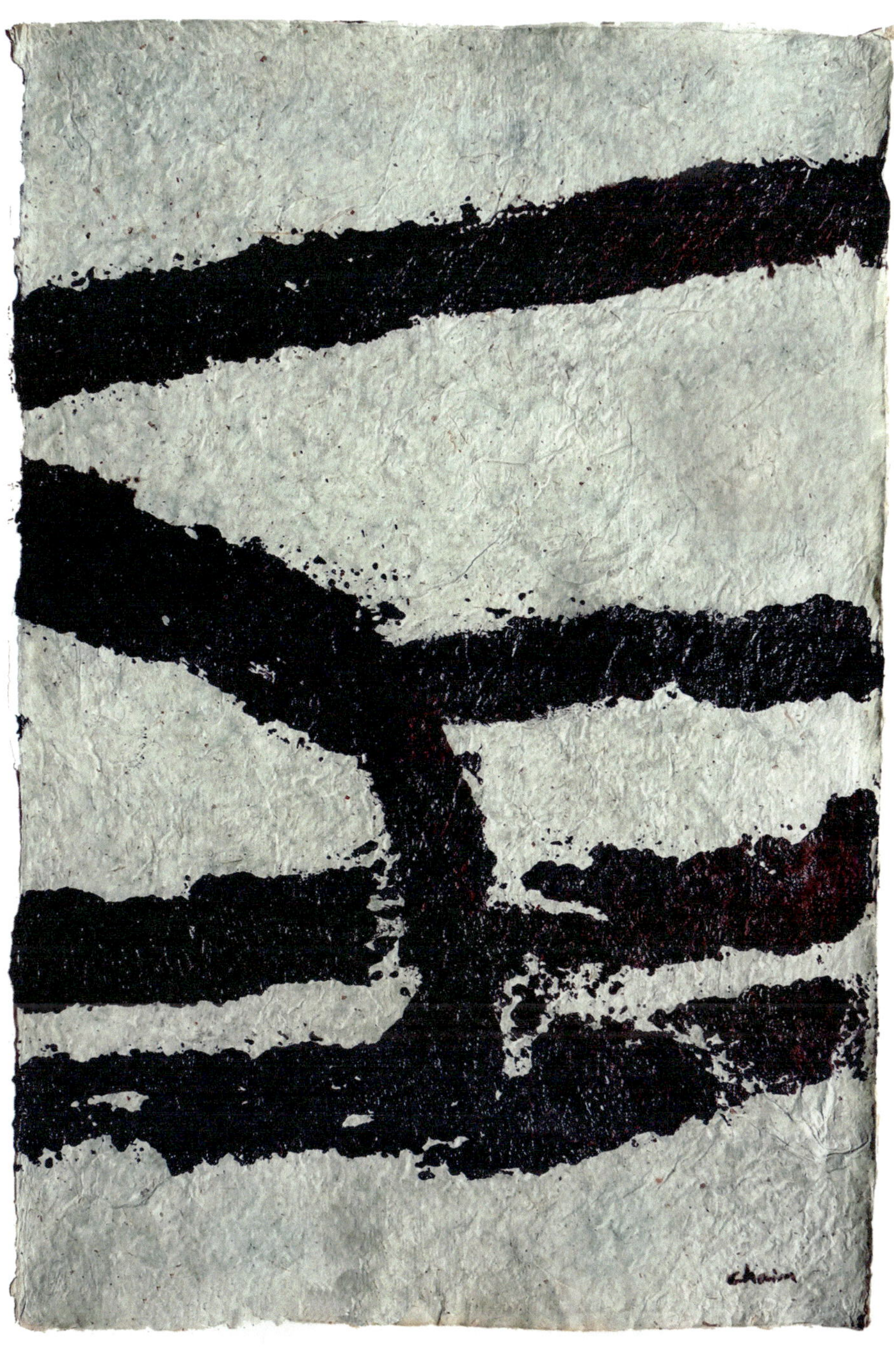

Roadwork Diptych (2014) 28 x 20 in. monoprint on handmade paper

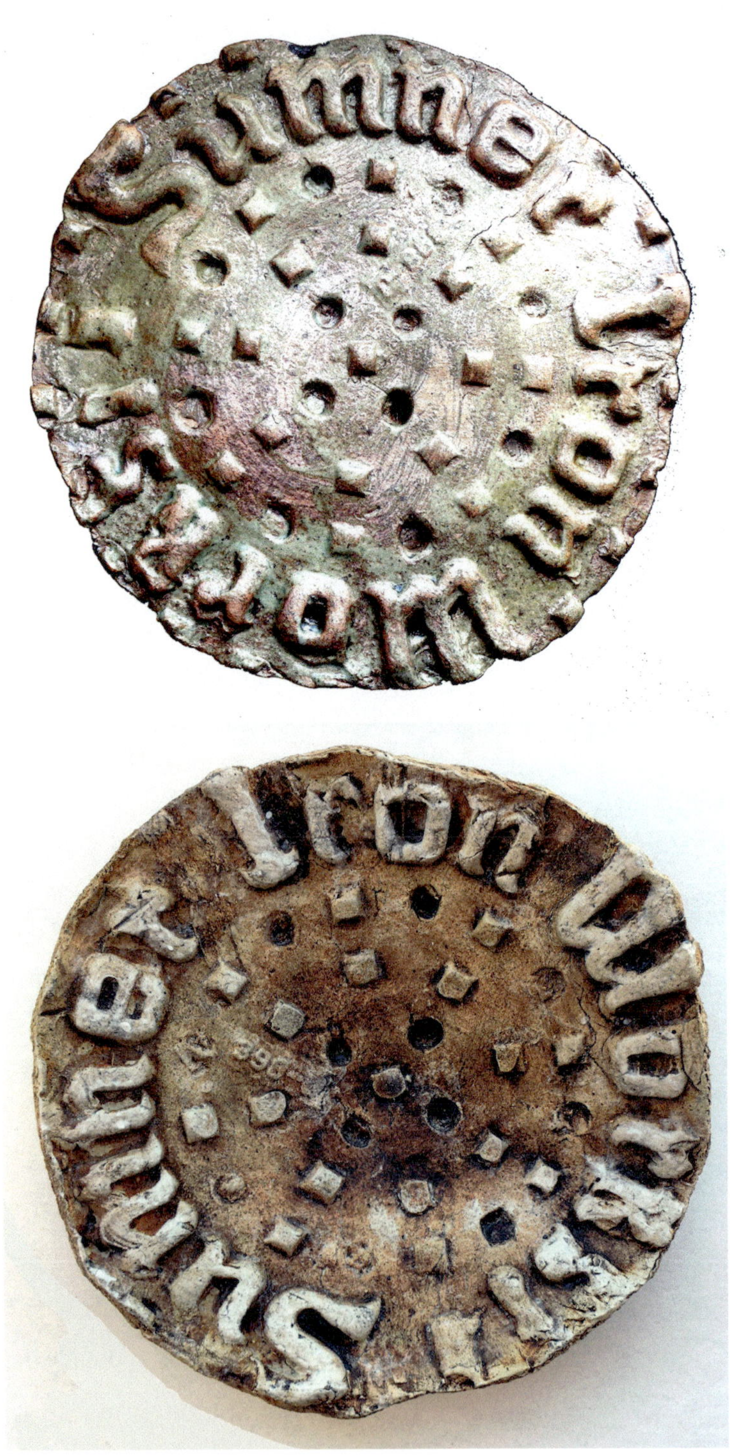

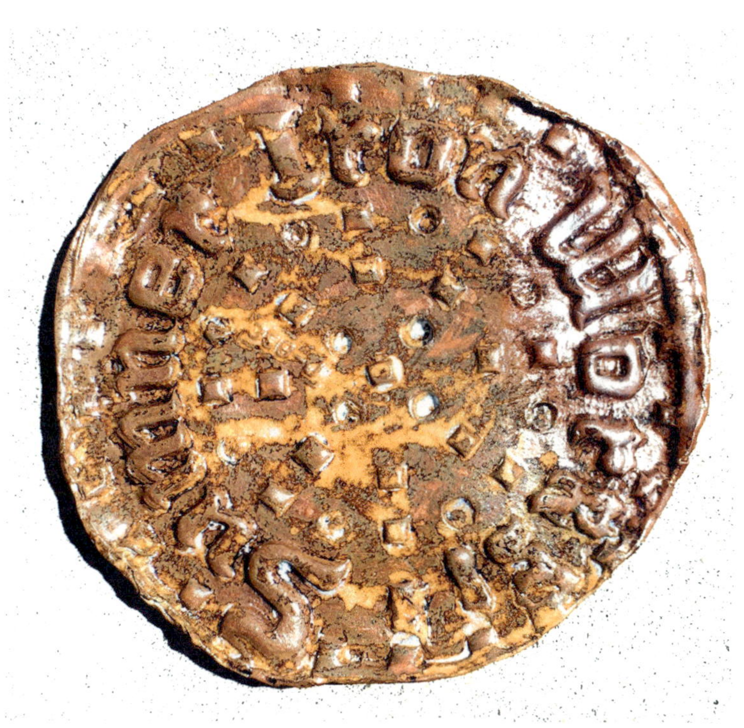

Sumner Iron Works Platters I, II, and III (2015) 17 in. diameter each

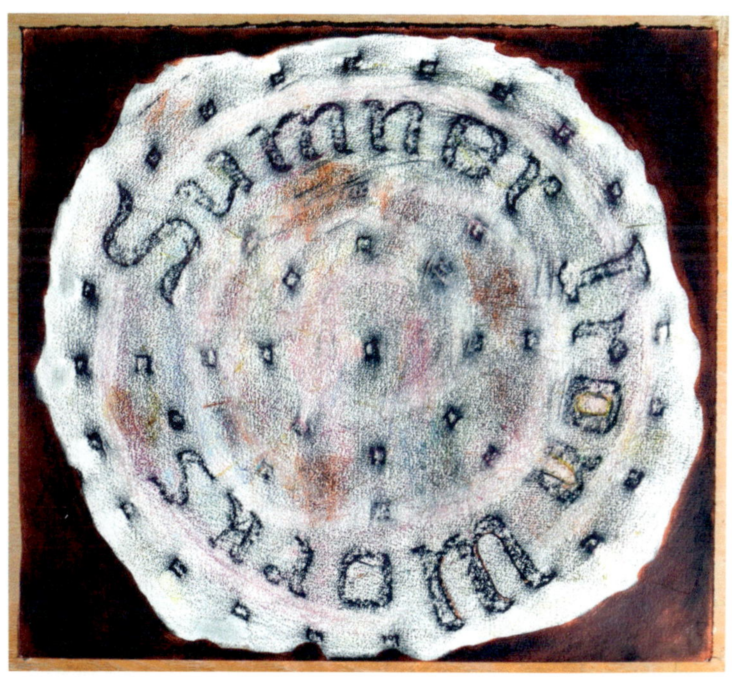

Sumner Iron Works (2016) crayon, oil pastels, acrylic, graphite on paper, 21 x 23 in.

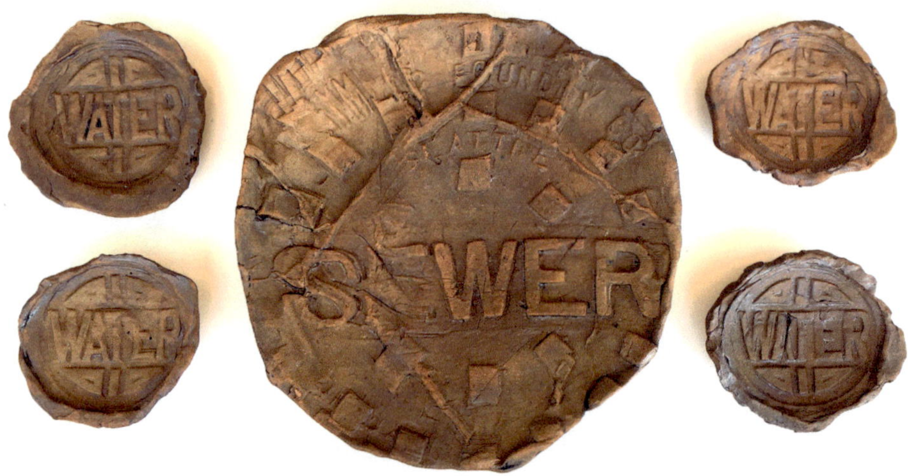

Water and Sewer Place Setting (2014) platter, 16 in. diameter, bowls, 8 in. diameter

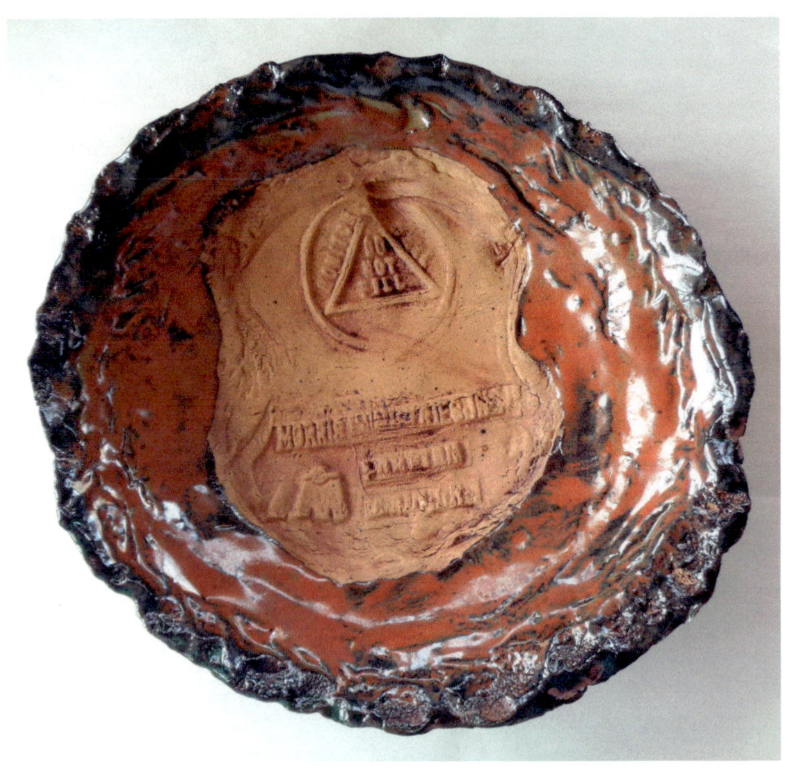

Do Not Fill (2016) ceramic bowl, 11 in. diameter

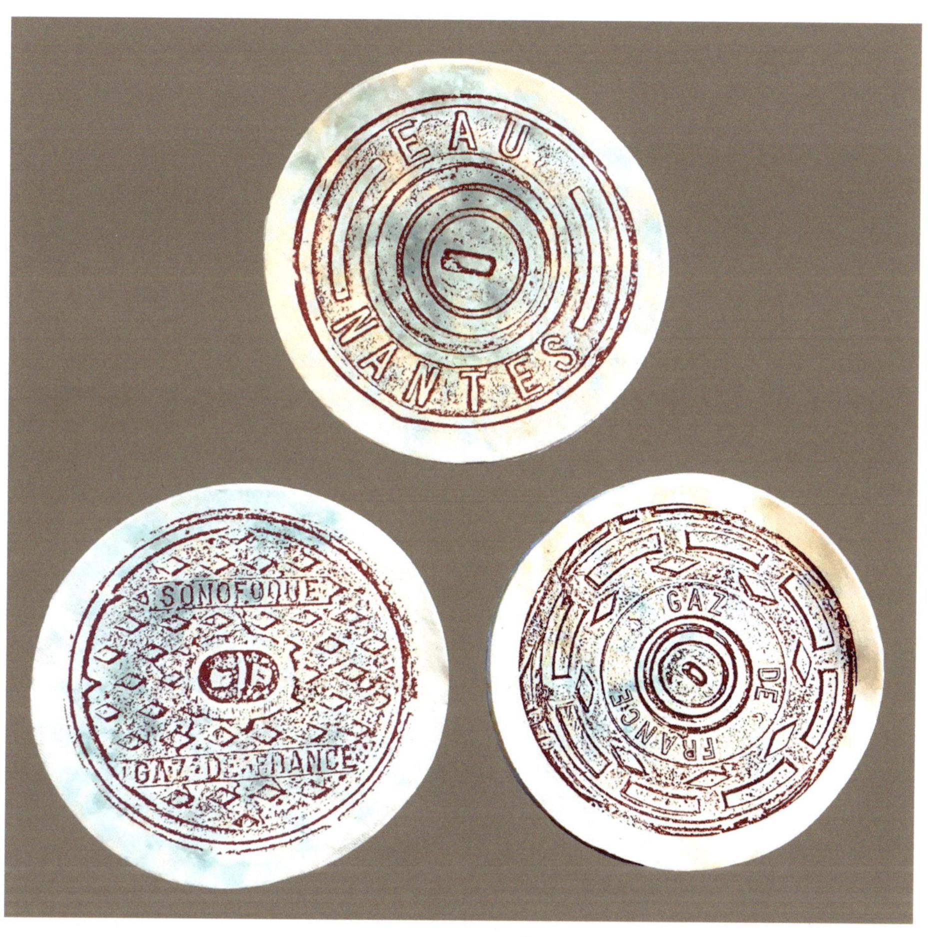

Water and Gas Utility Caps from Nantes, France (2016) Limoges porcelain tiles, 6 in.

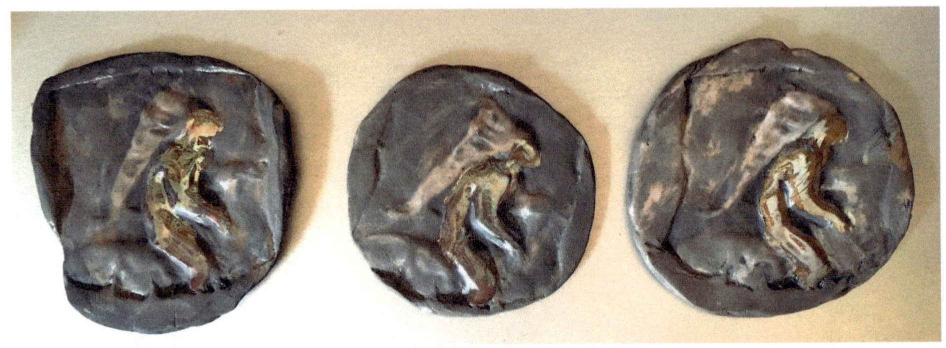

Indian Medallions (2017) raku fired clay, 8 – 9 in. diameter each

I made these from a mold of a section of a lamp post on Market Street in San Francisco. The 327 lamp posts each contain a circular bas relief of covered wagons, mountain lions, prospectors, and Indians. They were designed by Willis Polk in 1908, after the earthquake, for the city beautiful project. The boulevard is called the "Path of Gold." in memory of the gold rush or perhaps because of the gaslight that the lamps emitted.

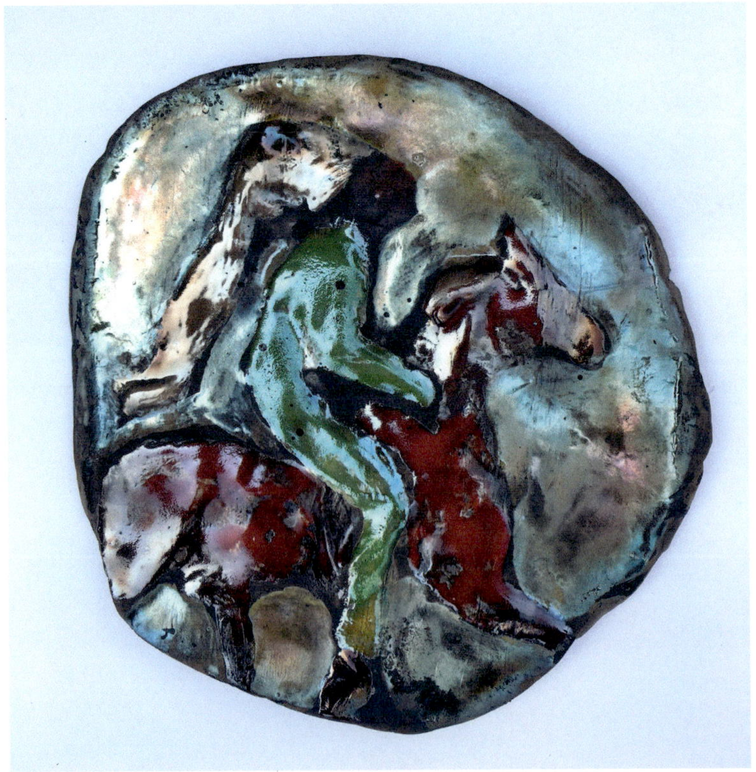

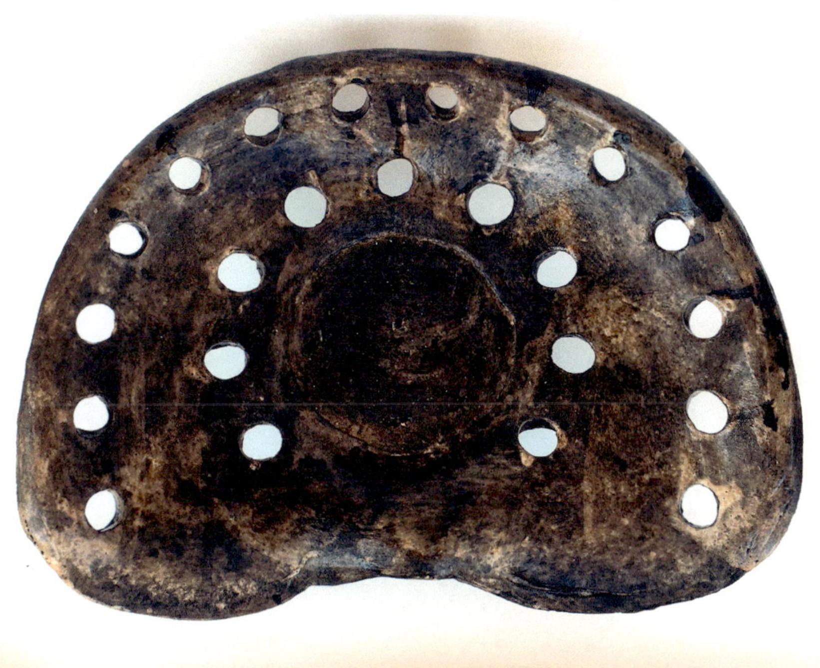

Tractor Seat (2017) Ceramics, 9 x 16 x 12 in. including pedestal

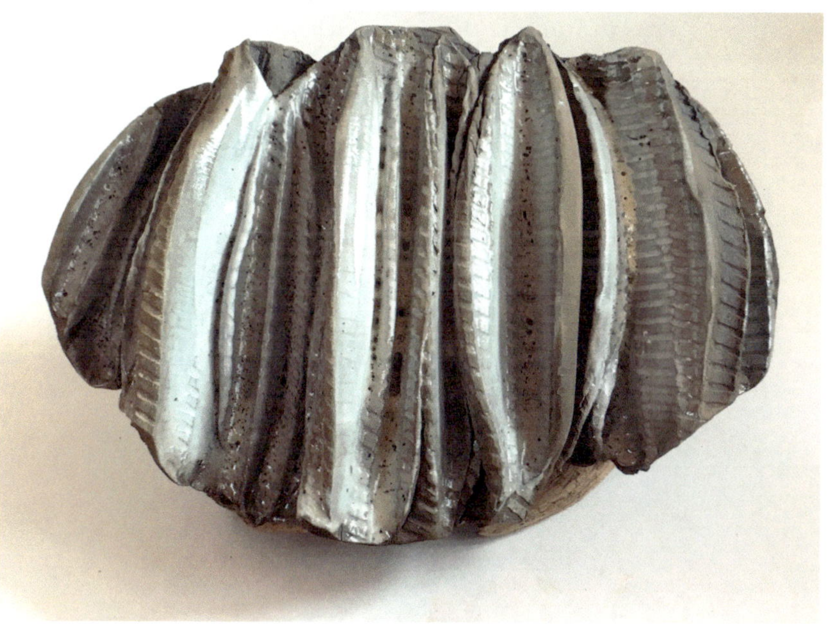

Rebar Sea Form (2016) raku fired clay mounted on driftwood, 8 x 12 x 8 in.

From the Fourth Estate (Bellingham Herald, August 16, 1949)

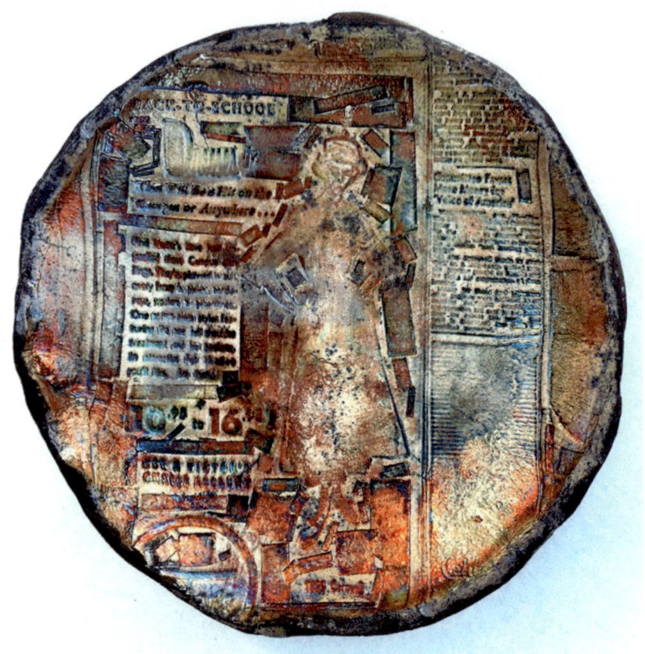

Back to School (2017) raku fired bowl, 10 x 9 ½ in.

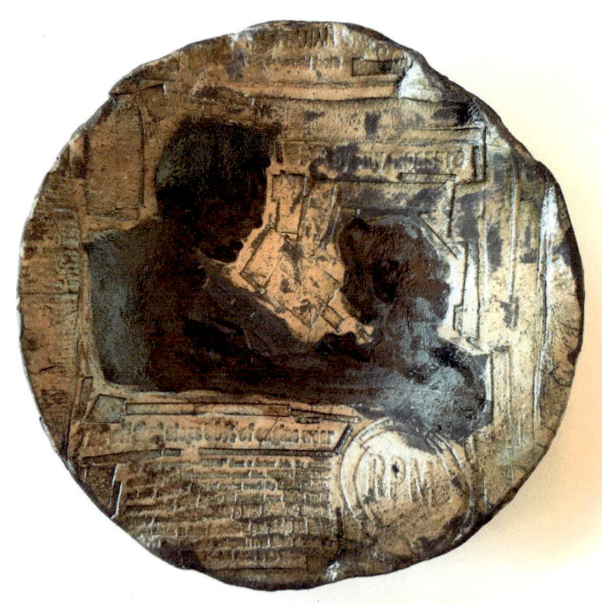

RPM Motor Oil Ad (2017) raku fired bowl, 10 x 10 in.

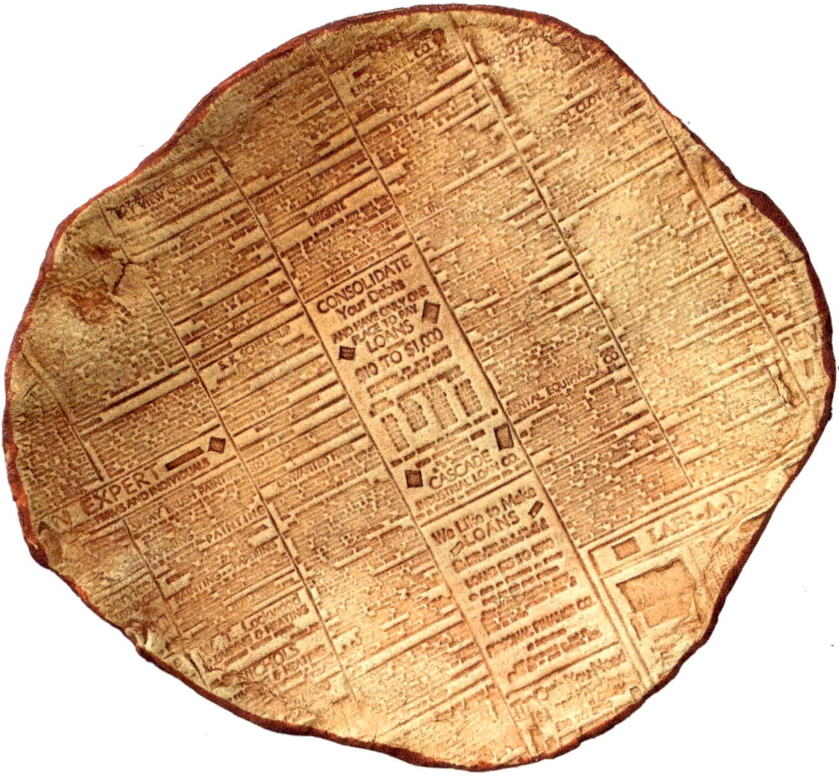

Consolidate Your Debts (2016) ceramic dish, 10 x 10 in.

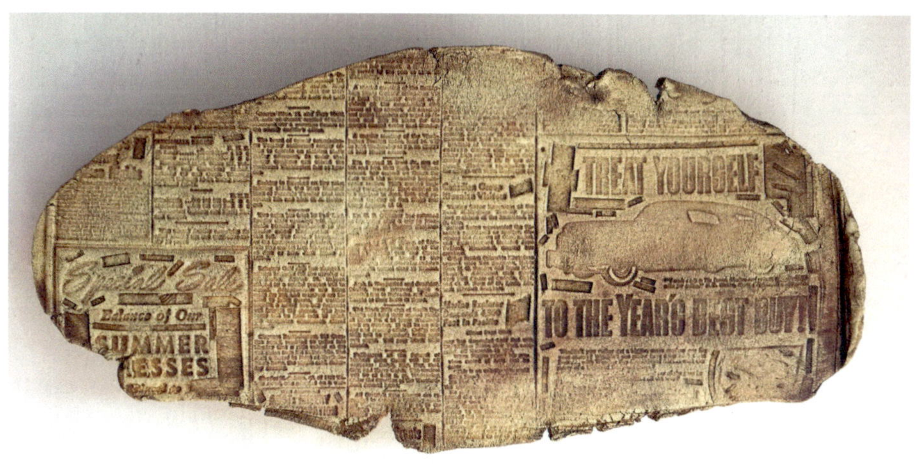

Treat Yourself (2016) ceramic plaque, 8 x 16 in.

Yizkor (Remembrance)

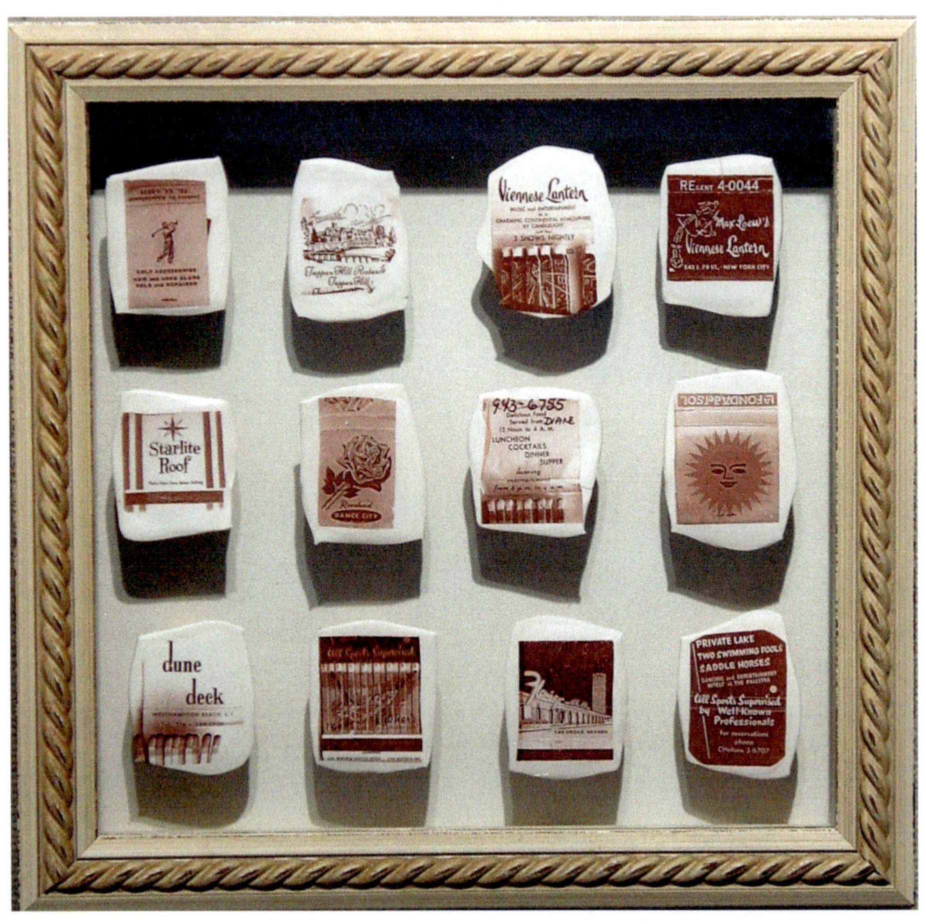

My Grandmother's Matchbook Collection (2007) mounted porcelain tiles, 15 x 15 in.

Note: I inherited my grandmother's Moroccan leather covered coffee table. I remembered as a child opening the drawer and going through her collection of matchbooks, mementos from various restaurants, hotels, and of course, Roseland dance palace. She had never wandered far from her apartment in the Bronx except for one trip west, by Greyhound. There she had collected a matchbook from the Kings Domain, a hotel in Lake Louise in British Columbia in which the entire phone number consists of only four digits.

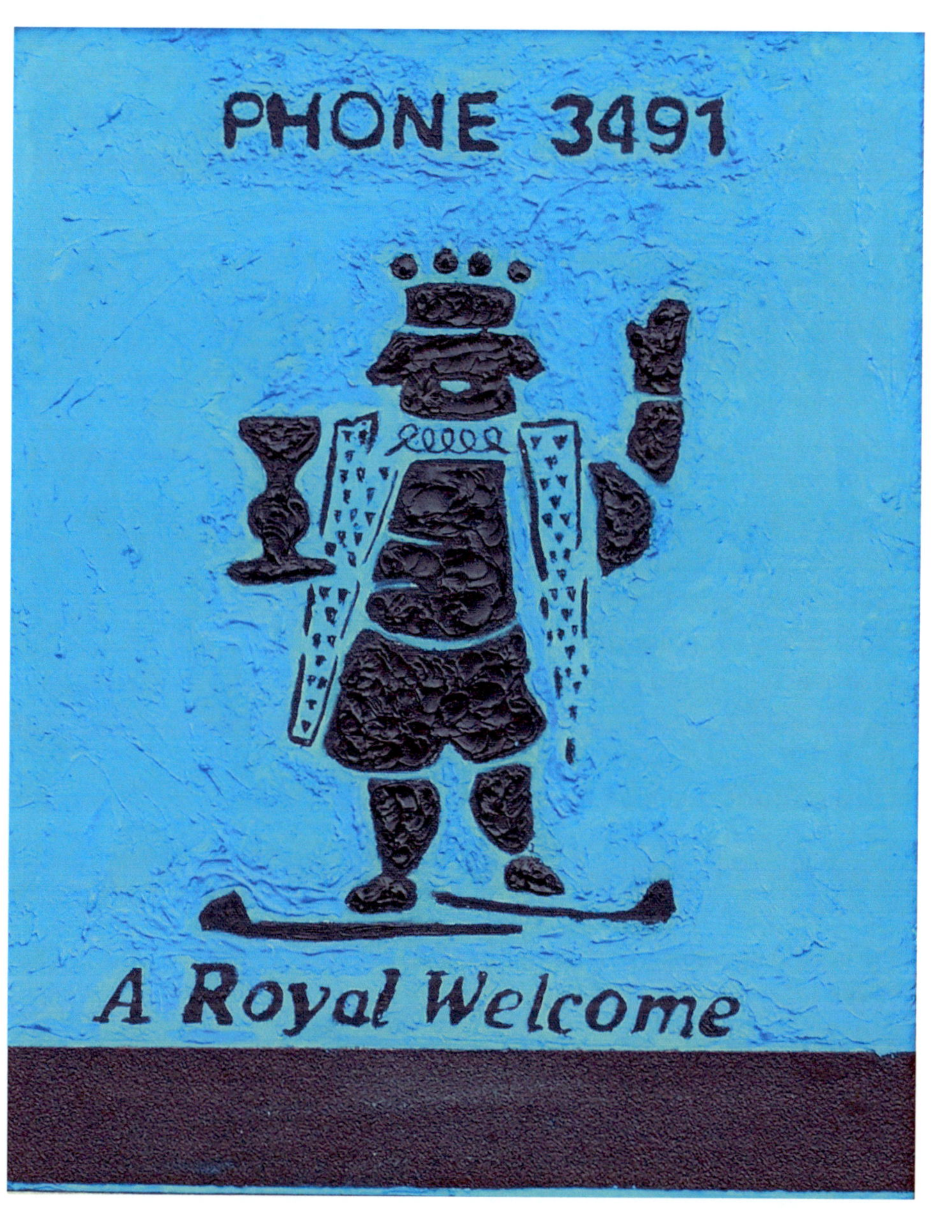

A Royal Welcome (2002) mixed-media with oils on canvas board, 20 x 16 in.

My Acting Career in Three Bit Parts

I

"Antigone" by Jean Anouilh. Dobbs Ferry H.S. Production, 1964

In my first role, freshman year
Age fourteen, a modern adaptation
of Antigone, I began my career
on stage. Stage right was my location
Throughout the play. I stood pretending
to write, although Anouilh, I thought,
Wrote the secretary's role without intention
To give a single line to relieve the ennui.
Fifty years later I search the script
and of such a part there is no mention,
Only the Page among the nondescript.
I was coached not to attract much attention.

Two small corrections need to be added.
Half a century, one may forget one's lines.
I had always thought my part had been padded
by the director; sometimes memory undermines
The truth. I see the Page I played
Did have a speaking part, five lines,
Each ending in "Sir," but mostly charade.
And there was a momentary exit and re-entry,
The page leaves the stage to usher Guard Number One,
Private Jonas. At least this bit of supplementary
information rounds out the picture before I am done.

Note: The French playwright Jean Anouilh's 1943 play "Antigone" is an
adaptation of Sophocles' classical drama. It is now recognized as a veiled
attack on Marshal Pétain's Vichy government.

II

"Line 300" Israel Television Production. 1996

An extra in a foreign film,
only it is not the film, but I
   who am foreign.
I play an attorney, without a line -
like an armless juggler.
I only feign conversation
with my colleague on the bench.
He inevitably responds, sotto voce,
"The matter remains to be clarified."
It is summer and we sweat
   under black robes -
windows sealed with filters,
no air conditioning or whirring fan,
while each witness recounts
the unfortunate circumstances
twenty or thirty times over.
Hell for a day with catered lunch.

Note: The Israeli television series concerned the trial of army officers and officials after the disappearance and death of two captured terrorists who hijacked a bus in 1984. Crossing into the Gaza Strip, Israeli soldiers were able to shoot out the tires and disable the bus ten miles north of the Egyptian border. Negotiations ensued. The hijackers demanded the release of 500 prisoners in return for the 40 passengers on the bus, whom they threatened to kill. The next morning the bus was stormed by special forces, killing two of the four hijackers. The remaining two were captured, taken to a nearby field and summarily executed under the orders of the head of Israeli internal intelligence known as Shin Bet. This was followed by a cover-up, an inquiry, and a trial, which became the subject of a documentary television series.

III

"Fiddler on the Roof" Light Opera Company of the Negev production, 2015

In a dressing room in Haifa I check my makeup, await my cue
Half a century since Antigone and my thespian debut.
Twenty years since my last role as a silent paraclete
Anyone can learn their lines, even a parakeet.
The fiddler on the roof moves his bow, pretends to play
We sit around the table making noise with nothing to say,
Speaking gibberish, getting drunk from glasses of air,
We all get up, dance across the stage like Fred Astaire
If he had been a drunken Jew back in the Russian pale
With his Jewish surname, Austerlitz, but Tradition didn't prevail.
Both quarry and hunter, I wear two hats, cloth and fur,
Cossack and Jew, bit part by bit, side by side, til transfer led
Some to America, some to destruction, some to the Promised Land.
We strut and fret and play out our roles,
       not always as we had planned.

Note: Fred Astaire was born Frederick Austerlitz. Astaire's father, Fritz Austerlitz, was born in Linz, Austria, to Jewish parents who had converted to Roman Catholicism.

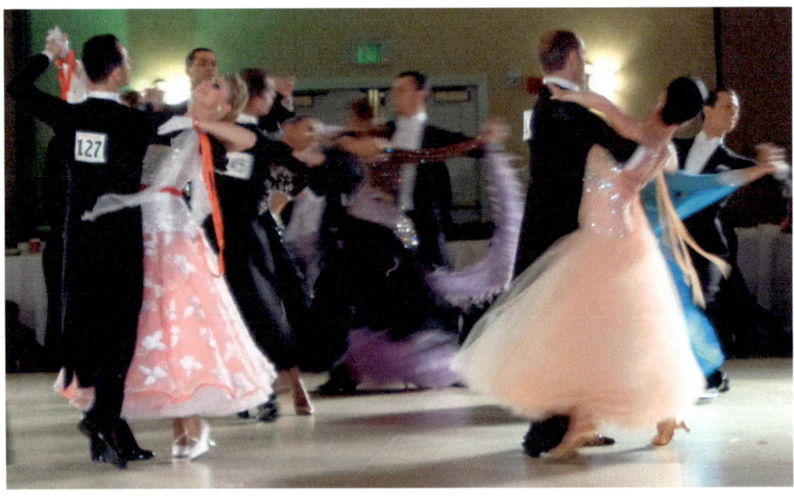

"Waltz and tango, slow and fast"

Death Watch for my Mother

It is not a strange thing to die,
But I cannot help but stare
As she lies sprawled, her face a mask,
Her cheeks gaunt, her nose prominent,
Her breasts like empty sacks, a scar
Marking where once her life was spared.
Yet in the end there is no escape.
I have never before seen her breasts bared
Bottle bred baby that I am.
She plucks at the sheets, at her skin, like Job.
Our love has been at one remove,
A continent or half the globe,
But life and so much more was given
And I the living still receiving
Soon I know will come the grieving.

Reduced not to dust but to ashes,
Now a week has gone and she has passed.
In the hotel ballroom they dance their dances,
Waltz and tango, slow and fast.
"You pays your money, you takes your chances"
Not seeing the number on our back
As it is judged who leaves the floor
(Will she meet her mother in Roseland Palace?)
And if we span three score or more
To drink to the dregs from a golden chalice.

Note: Roseland Ballroom was a dance and music hall in New York City. It opened in 1917 and closed in 2014. My maternal grandmother, Sabina, won several trophies for dance contests there, including one for the tango.

I and Thou

Are you there?
Are you Thou?
Are you eternally
Here and now?
 I used to believe,
I used to by rote.
If you know my server
Than drop me a note.
I'm not an observer
I'm not on my knees.
I don't have that fervor
but do aim to please.
I think when we started
the waters were parted
and you had outsmarted
the powers that be.
But the tides were a changing
and we were exchanging
a covenant or two,
an old and a new.
It's not really rejection,
I'm not into perfection; I mean
it's the process that
drives the machine.
I've heard you're a verb
which I think is superb -
present perfect continuous,
I take it.
But still undefined,
renewing my mind renewing
the world before we break it.

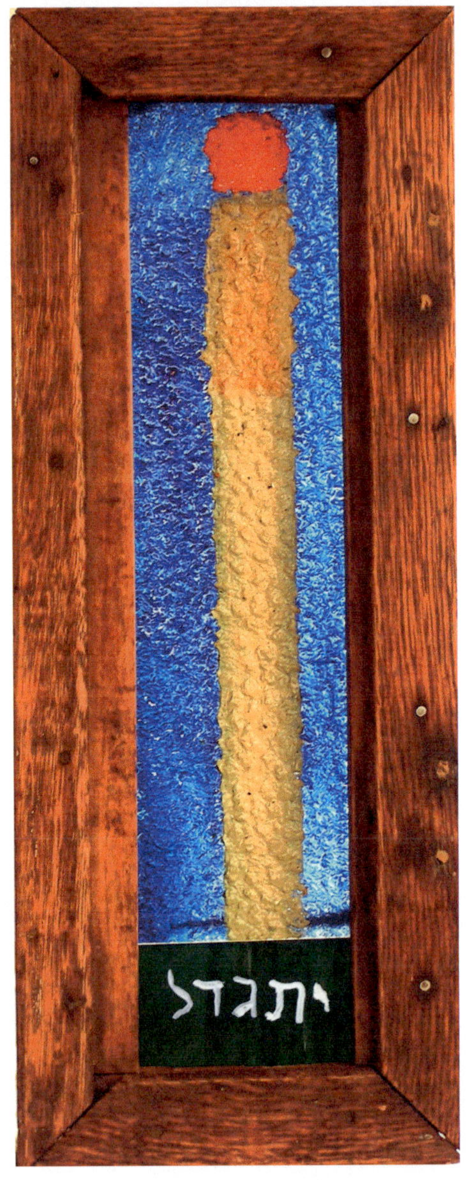

Yitgadol (2007) oil on glass, 14 x 6 in.

Note: *"Yitgadol" (Magnified) is the first word of the Kaddish prayer which demarcates each segment of a Jewish prayer service. It is also repeated as the Mourners' Kaddish.*

A Moment of Silence

Gate seven JFK nine eleven seventeen
The second silence scarcely observed
Not like the first which was unreserved
The President appears on the TV screen

Taps for the victims or for what ended that day
We know what is coming and while we wait
Life goes on at the departure gate
We all saw it live or on instant replay

As hurricanes rage and fires burn
We're flying back into the eye of the storm
Have a safe trip, friends and neighbors warn
We stop over in Britain before our return

We've been following Mary Queen of Scots
Caught in the years of religious war
That spanned one hundred and twenty-four
Bartholomew's Day Massacre, the Gunpowder Plot

Tomorrow it's on to Tel Aviv
A drive to our home in Ashkelon
Our Hundred Years War is off and on
Presently it seems we have a reprieve

So before we fly into the eye of the storm
A bombing in London makes them increase
Their security measures as they check each valise
What once was unthinkable has become the norm

Our Town

I have a friend of Norwegian extraction
In fact I have two, maybe a few.
One might suppose a mutual attraction
Between Norwegians and Jews.
There are differences in how they express
   their views. In a typical interaction
The Norwegian chews his words
   and then swallows them; the Jew
Just spits them out, and gestures too.

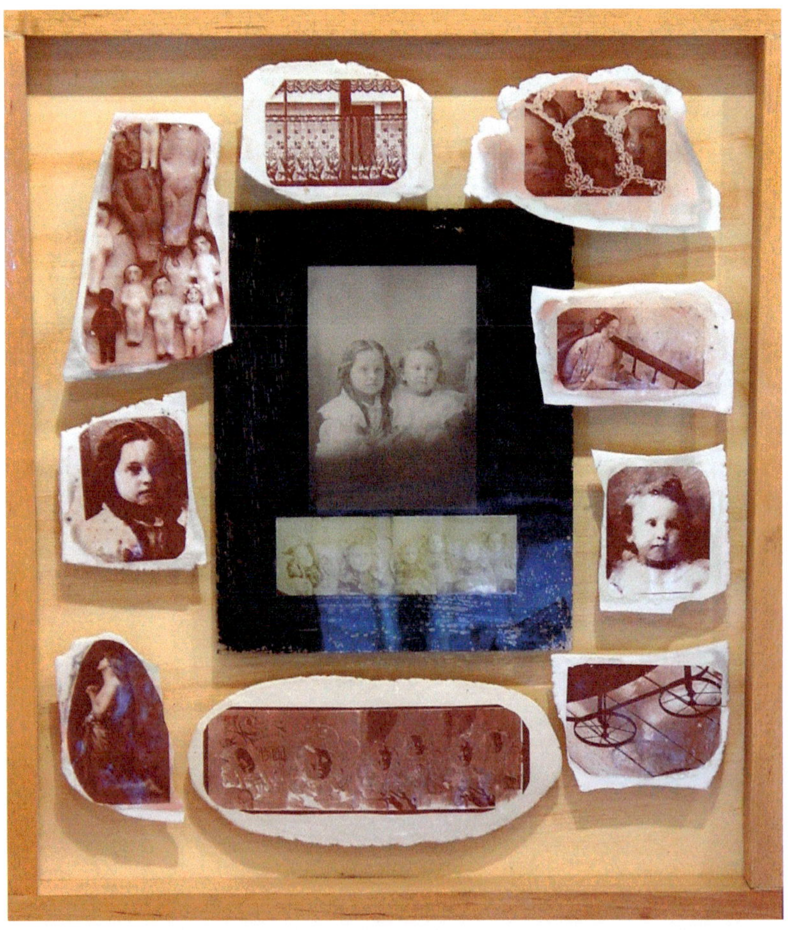

Our Town (2012) Antique Ambrotype on glass, porcelain tiles, 21 x 18 in.

Saks off Fifth

Waiting in the shoe department while she tries on skirts.
Saks is where my mother used to buy my slacks and shirts
Those "Happy Days" when teens wore jeans
    to look like Marlon Brando.
The salesman in baggy pants, his name was Mr. Blando
I still recall his white mustache, as they quietly conspired
If he was then as old as me, he would have been retired.

Saks OFF Fifth on Market Street, a knock-off of itself
Waiting patiently for my wife as she meanders shelf to shelf
Music thrumming from the ceiling into every niche
Elevator dings in middle C proves I have perfect pitch.
The ventilation's steady hum into this bargain basement
Reminds me of how far we've come
    – department store's debasement.

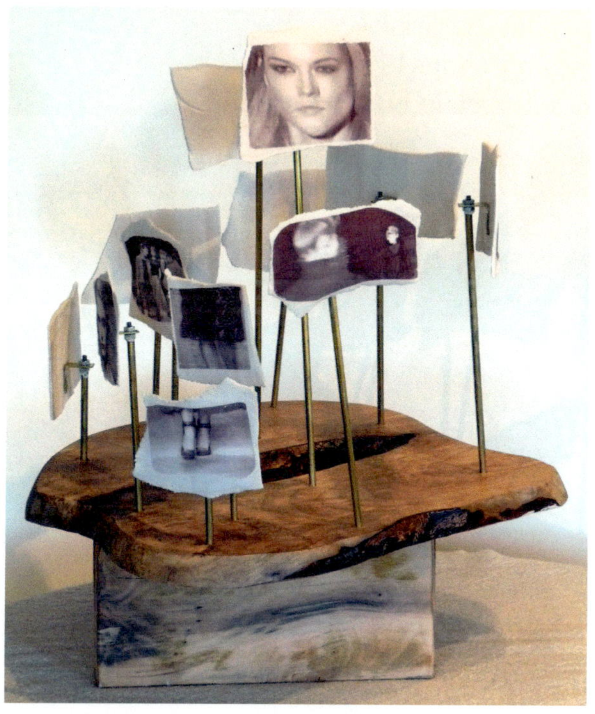

Catwalk (2010) porcelain, wood, brass (revolves with electric motor) 22 x 17 x 17 in.

Rivers and Springs (from *American Scrolls*, Dekel Press, 2000)

In a land divided by rivers we traveled,
Sometimes floating on waters named
With the Indian names in languages lost
Or nearly lost, an entire continent "tamed."

Starting in Aripeka, Seminole for bird,
Drifting down the Weeki Wachee,
Meaning little spring or winding river,
We followed the mermaid manatee.

Homosassa, "the place of many pepper plants"
In the tongue of the native Creek -
Flamingo, pelican, anahinga,
And spoonbill with a shovellike beak.

And three snowy egrets reflected in a pool
Lifted out of a Chinese scroll
White as snow and wings like lace
As delicate as a porcelain bowl.

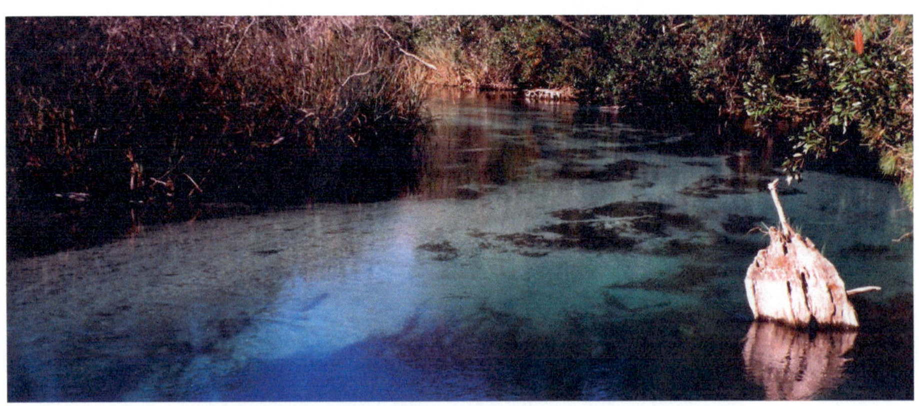

Homosassa River, Florida

The Frontier (from *Songs from the Territories*, Dekel Press, 2000)

I mourn the loss of frontier.
It is what keeps us sane.
Without it, we go out to convert the world
To our collective god or brand name.
Not that everyone should live there,
Just that it exists,
Something as yet unspoiled, bare
Of all but necessity.
I mourn the loss of frontier,
Where the outcast, outlaw, fortune seeker
Can have a clean slate
With inducement to settle and cultivate.

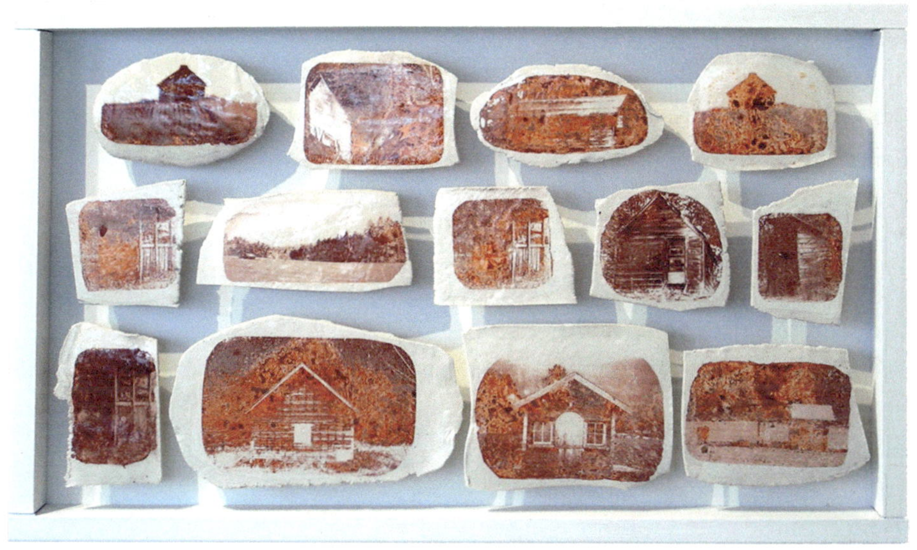

The End of the American Frontier (2007) porcelain tiles, 19 x 24 x 2 in.

In his thesis, "The Significance of the Frontier in American History," (1893) Frederick Jackson Turner expressed concern over the disappearance of the land frontier. He attributed the character of our institutions to the changes involved *"in crossing a continent, in winning a wilderness, and in developing at each area of this progress out of the primitive economic and political conditions of the frontier into the complexity of city life."*

The Preacher

I

All is vain the preacher is sayin'
What do you gain from your sweat and strain
Don't wrack your brain, it's all in vain,
Too much wisdom will only bring pain.

Once you had your fill of wine, women, and song
Preach me the difference between right and wrong.

Think you'll live forever, that's insanity
We share the same fate with all humanity
So best to keep silent from inanity
And to also to refrain from profanity.

Pie in the sky or mud in your eye
No use worryin' 'bout the by and by.
Nothing is new under the sun
When all's said and done it's all been said and done.
Enjoy your work, try and have some fun
And remember that two are better than one.

II

It doesn't matter where we're from
We're all going to the same place,
Heaven, Sheol, or Elysium
Six feet under or outer space

Which makes me wonder as I wander
Like John Jacob Niles in his song
To meditate on "over yonder"
Or just try to tell what's right and wrong.

I'm goin' home to meet my mother
I'm goin' home to meet my dad
I'm goin' home to meet my sister
Or just remember good times we had.

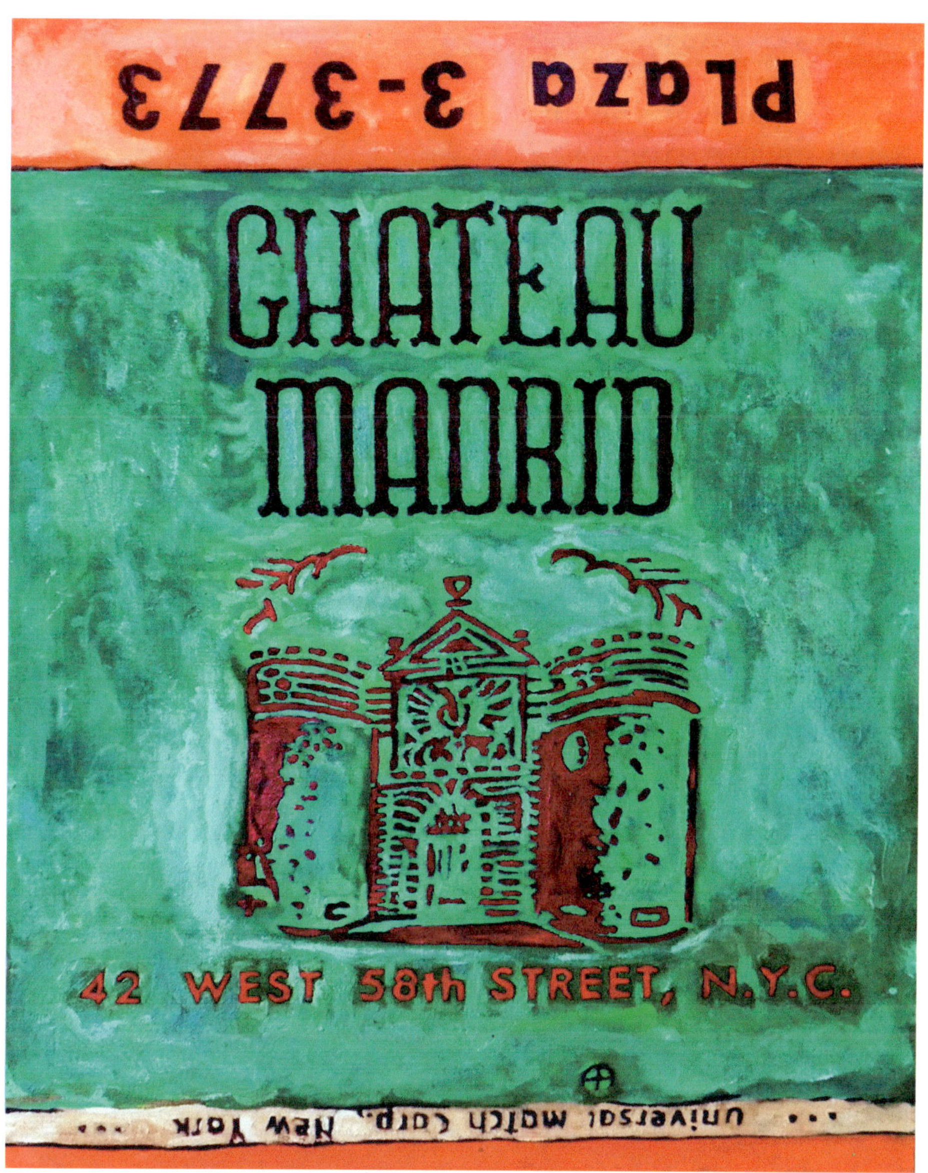

Chateau Madrid (2011) oil on linen, 37 x 24 in.

No Place Like Home

An anthropomorphic fox cavorts
  on the in-flight screen
But I'm plugged into a classical mix
Drinking Snappy Tom on the rocks.
Now I know what it means,
  "I get no kicks in a plane."
The two page spread which I stain
  with ink says Lancôme
But makes me think,
    there's no place like home.

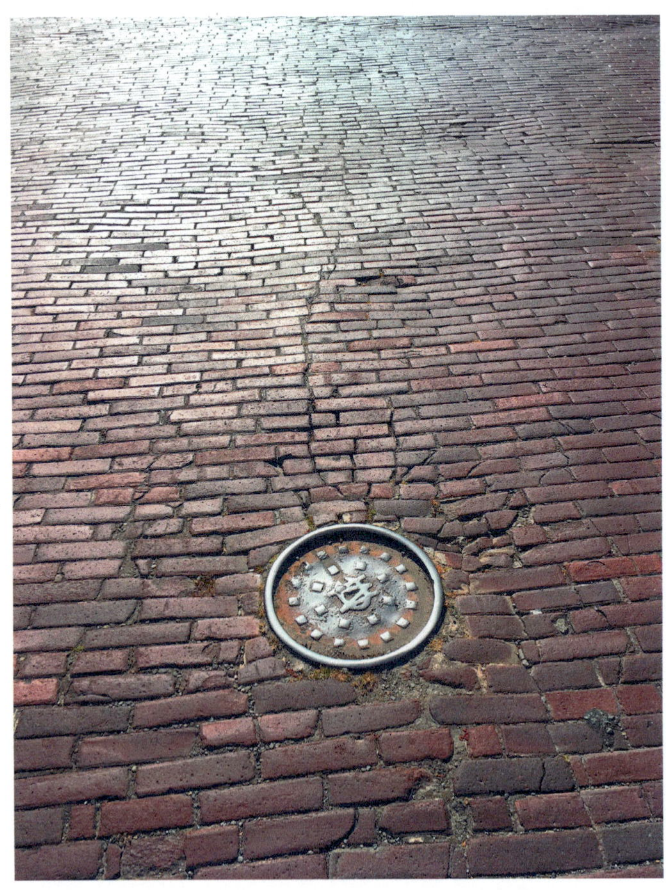

Main Street, Stanwood, WA

Lyrics

(songs can be streamed or downloaded at cdbaby.com/chaimbezalel)

One Foot Stuck in the Romantic Age

One Foot Stuck in the Romantic Age, too late now to die young,
Like Keats and Shelley, James Dean and Grace Kelly.
For me it's been a pretty long run.
Maybe you get to a certain age, you learn a lot of stuff.
I'm just a late bloomer, a baby boomer,
I'm tellin' ya' straight off the cuff.
Maybe we've entered a different stage
Where people don't lead from the heart,
But follow their heads, playing the odds instead
Before they're even ready to start.

One foot stuck in the Romantic Age, I still believe in belief,
If not for me then for those who can be like the lilies of the field.
In brief, somewhere between a Romantic and just an average Joe
A working stiff on the graveyard shift with an hour and a half to go.
But hey, I'm not a clock-watcher, and it's not like I'm not having fun.
Inviting the muse in can be mighty amusin'
As long as your not under the gun.

One foot stuck in the Romantic Age, one more dragon to slay.
I'll take the field with a sword and a shield,
Well tomorrow if not today
One foot stuck in the Romantic Age and one in the modern world.
Don't mean to straddle, just choose my battle
With flag held high and unfurled
Maybe I'm a Don Quixote or maybe just his sidekick
Disbelief suspended till the story's ended, or the candle's
     to the end of the wick.

The Simple Son

Somewhere in the heavenlies a voice cries out when a match is made
This one for that one, the voice calls out, so is is said.
You may think that there are more important things to do
Than cry out loud upon a cloud concerning me and you.

You gaze at the sky while I'm lying, asleep in the night
Some stars are being born and some dying,
By the time we see their light.

Do you think that everything follows a plan world without end.
Do you think that there is some invisible hand, not just pretend,
Working out the good in all to triumph over the wrong.
Is that the thing you want to sing together in this song.

I don't have the answer; there were times I thought I did.
Sometimes truth is like a dancer,
Seven veils to keep her hid.

Somewhere inside me a voice explains we are each a star
Giving out the light that we contain, whether near or far.
One by one or sometimes in a constellation's tow
Through a glass we see if at all darkly where we come from,
   where we go.

As we sit around the table. As we each lift up our glass,
I'm like the simple son in the fable,
  or the one who doesn't know how to ask.

*Note: "Forty days before conception, a heavenly voice calls out: 'The
daughter of so-and-so to so-and-so.'" - from Sotah 2a Talmud*

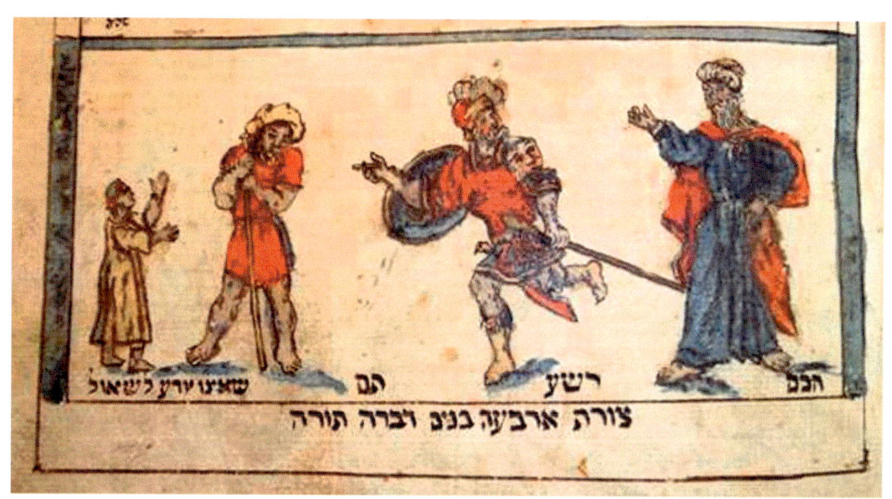

The Four Sons from a Haggadah printed in Amsterdam in 1695

The following passage comes from the Haggadah which is read at the table while observing the Passover feast: *"The Torah refers to four sons: One wise, one wicked, one simple and one who does not know how to ask."* The picture depicts them in the same order, right to left.

Frozen in Time

Like a deer blinded in the headlights
Like a blizzard in the state of Maine
Like Frosty the Snowman, Nanook of the North
Or Rosebud from Citizen Kane
Like an insect trapped in the amber
Or a spaceman at the speed of light
Never getting older
As long as he remains in flight

Chorus:
Frozen in time, frozen in time
As long as we're moving together
We are frozen in time

Well it doesn't take an Einstein
To talk about relativity
We're all relating to someone
Like the birds are relating to the bees
Or maybe it's the birds relating to the birds
And the bees relating to the bees
Somehow I go a feeling
You could be relating with me

Chorus

Like old Ponce de Leon
Searching for the fountain of youth
He would've saved himself a lot of time
If he'd only known the truth
That we're all getting older and some are getting wise
To what is at the core
Two bodies moving in space and time
Are all the matter and energy's for

Chorus

Karen

Flying up where the air is clear
Climbing into the blue
Smiling without a thing to fear
I'll remember you

And if sometimes I wasn't there
Still I tried to take your part
If you thought I didn't care
Still you broke my heart

Wanting what you couldn't even name
Crying out tears of rage
Reaching to grasp it just the same
I'll remember you

And then one day you flew away
Climbing into the setting sun
Night gently following the day
Looking for the lights to show the way

You were so close and yet so far
Landing lights lit up in view
Falling just like a falling star
I'll remember you

Oh my sister oh so sad and brave'
Oh so foolish and so wise
I could love you but I could not save
Your life or see it through your eyes

*from The New York Daily News,Sept. 4, 2005: "A Brooklyn psychologist
was identified yesterday as the pilot killed when her small plane crashed
near Teterboro Airport Friday night."*

Life in the Slow Lane

Living incognito on our isle of bliss
Leaving all the world behind, can't it be like this
The tide goes out and the tide comes in
Apple tree blossoms and the summer begins

Chorus:
That's life in the slow lane with you babe
That's life in the slow lane
I'll live a lot longer with you babe
I wanna live a lot longer with you.

Do you want to read awhile till we close our eyes
We can talk tomorrow about our whats and whys
The twilight goes on till almost midnight
But we can turn out the light are you sleepy now - quite.

Chorus

I've been around the world and I've been to London too
The sunset in Jerusalem is really quite a view
Some days I wake up and don't know where I'm at
Some say that home is wherever you hang your hat.

Chorus

I do not care about fortune or fame
I do not care if they ever know my name
I do not want to try any new toothpaste
Living with anyone else would be a waste.

The Sky is not Falling

The sky is not falling though prophets of doom are calling
That maybe it will.
Apocalypse is stalling which some might find appalling
But we still have time to kill

Let's settle in for the duration you can change the station
I've had my fill.
The planet may warm more than the norm
So why don't we chill.

The Dow may keep dropping if shoppers stop shopping
Like they did in the boom.
It may be a bear but I really don't care
To share in the gloom.
Don't try to alarm me the Salvation Army
Has plenty of room
And if they insist and I have to enlist
I can still push a broom.

If they tell you that we're going straight to hell in a handbasket
Well, them's the brakes.
Sometimes I can almost smell the sulphur see the burning lake.
If you fall down a well you can yell but still there's one way to take
That is higher, don't expire or tire though it's dire and you're stuck in
    the mire and it's down to the wire
There's much too much at stake.

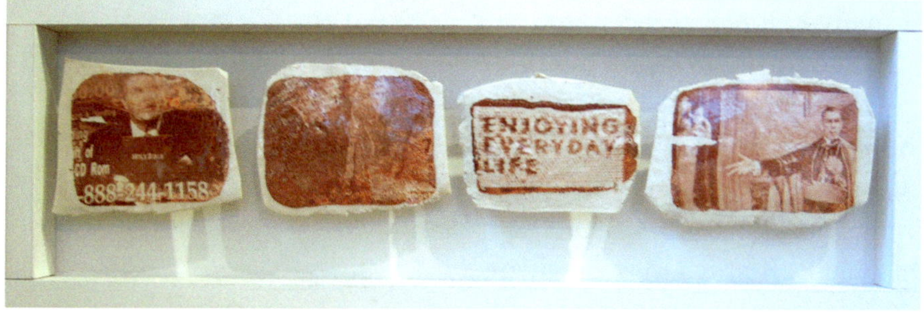

TV Evangelists (2006) mounted porcelain tiles, 7 x 21 x 3 in.

Song for Henri Rousseau

He was an ordinary man
A customs clerk somewhere in France
Till he retired at forty-nine
He lived a life inside his mind

He never left his native land
To paint what he had never seen
The sleeping gypsy in the sand
The world suspended in a dream

He holds a staff still in his hand
A lion sniffs around his head
Is he asleep or just pretend
His lute is silent as the dead

The moon is watching from the sky
The stars are peering through the dawn
The lion gazes with his eye
The gypsy sleeps until the morn

And there is even more to tell
The mountains rising from the plain
They play their part they cast their spell
A world where nothing is mundane

The coat he wears like Joseph's own
Also a dreamer he was called
Of many colors it was sewn
Will it be torn will he be mauled?

They say that always in the dream
Each thing you see is only you
Things are not always what they seem
Or what at first we may construe

A nude reclining on a chair
Where jungle vegetation grows
The creatures deep within all stare
Regarding Henri Rousseau

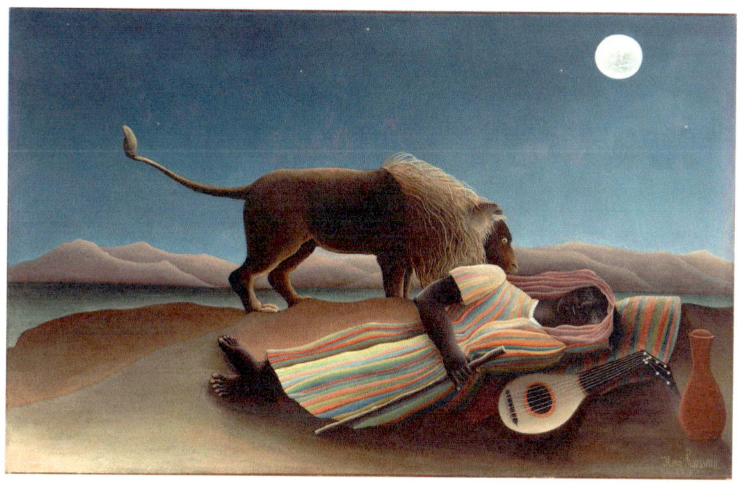

The Sleeping Gypsy, Henri Rousseau (collection Museum of Modern Art)

(Both images are "slavish" photographic reproductions and in the public domain under the ruling in Bridgeman Art Library v. Corel Corp.)

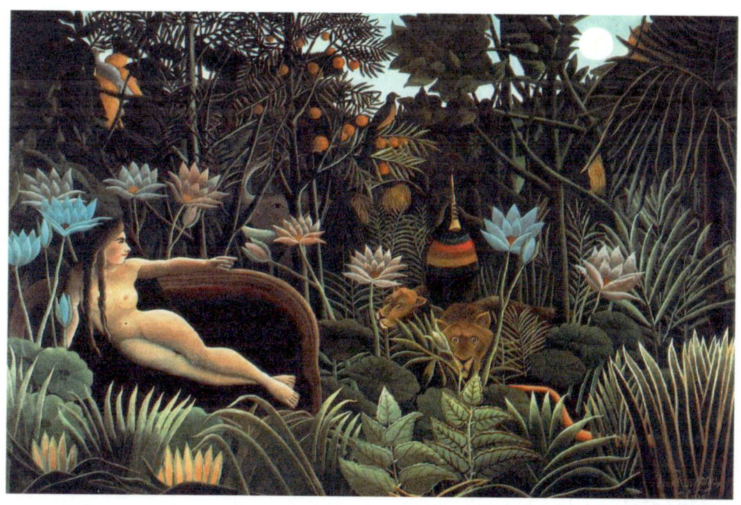

The Dream, Henri Rousseau (collection Museum of Modern Art)

Man Overboard

Man overboard, man overboard
Over the top and over the hill
A little overbearing but I love you still
Man overboard

Can I keep on swimming
Will I reach the shore
Tell me if you're out there
I can't wait much more

Man overboard, man overboard
Over the limit and over the line
Well shiver me timbers I'm soaking in brine
Man overboard

Water water everywhere
But not a drop to drink
Should I just go under
I know I'm on the brink

Man overboard, man overboard
Over the rainbow and over the moon
Over my head if they don't get here soon
Man overboard

I guess that we're all wondering
How this story ends
Will somebody save my soul
Before I get the bends

Man overboard, man overboard
It's not over till it's over and the fat lady sings
Then it's over in the clover with a pitchfork or wings
Man overboard

Who will go by fire
Who will go by flood
We can't live forever
We're only flesh and blood.

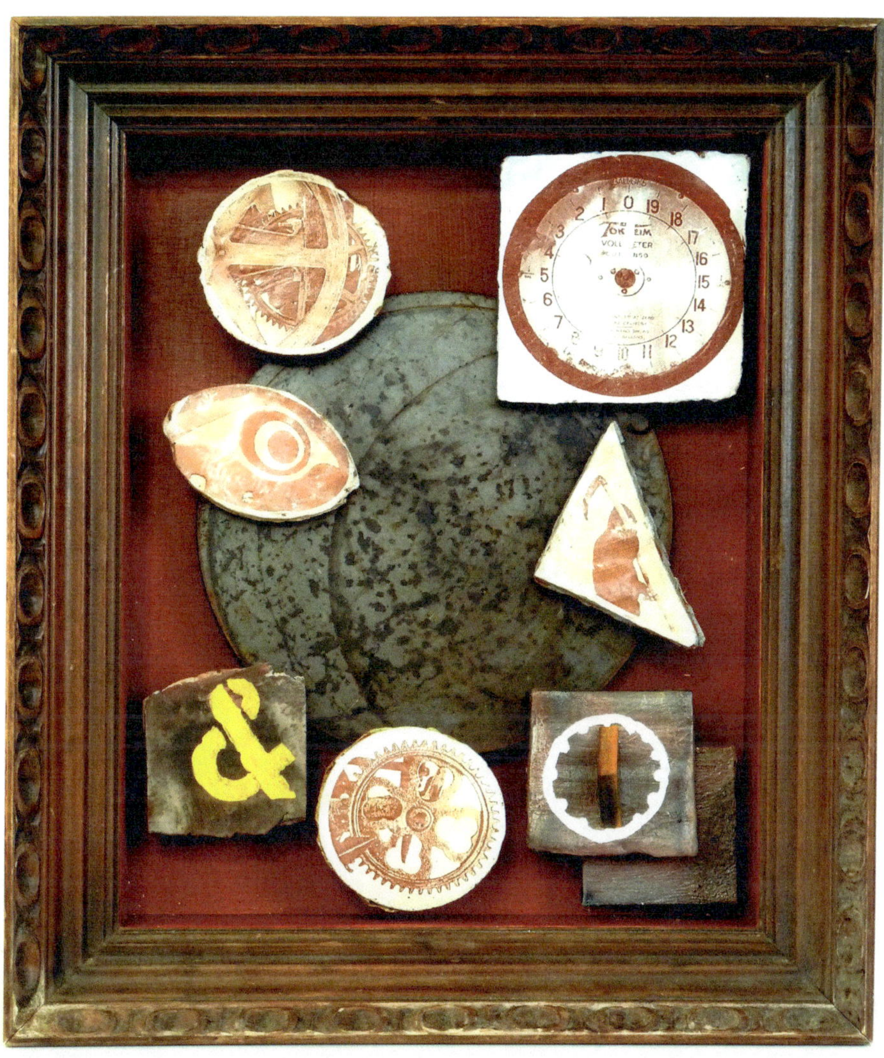

Time & Tide (2012) assemblage with steel and ceramics in shadowbox, 25 x 21 x 6 in.

I Don't Sing For Money

I don't sing for money, that's not my gig
Throw some coins in the jukebox if that's what you dig
I ain't no idol with perfect pitch
Ain't got no pitchman to help me strike it rich.

I'm just a guy who sings for free
Still singing commercials from 1953
Oh no, here it comes again
They went out of business, I don't know when

Brusha brusha brusha new Ipana toothpaste
Brusha brusha brusha, it's dandy for your teeth.

Don't reach for your wallet, I don't need your dough
All I want is to go bo-bo-bodio-doh.
And if you need me, tell you where I'm gonna be
Tin Pan Alley General Delivery.

I don't sing for money, that's not my gig
Throw some coins in the jukebox if that's what you dig.

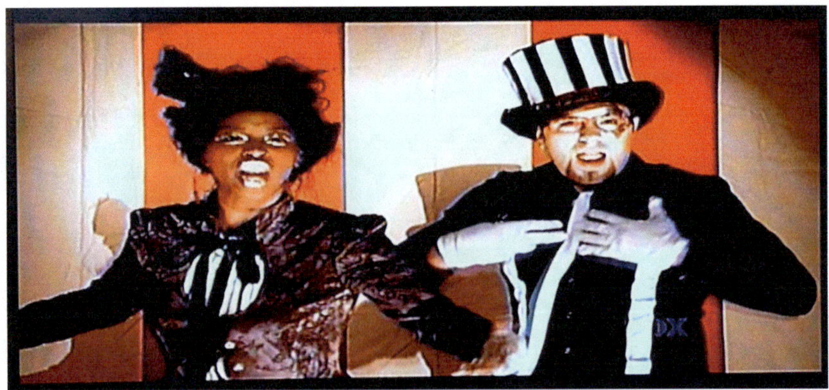

"I ain't no idol with perfect pitch"

Everything is Mixed

Everything is mixed
Don't try to get it fixed
You'll never get your kicks that way
Don't try to be so pure
You never can be sure
And there's always something more to say.

You are not perfect nor am I
Needless to expand
But the equation you and I
Leads to something grand

Everything's a blend
Don't try to comprehend
It's easier my friend that way
It's one day at a time
That's the reason and the rhyme
If you're OK then I'm OK

We may not live forevermore
Love may not extend
Beyond however long we may endure
But I'm sure it's till the end.

Repeat 1st stanza

Josephina *(a tango)*

When I met her she was almost pretty
But she was just over the hill
She was thirty-three and I was twenty
And she was moving in for the kill

She had no milk of human kindness
But a wit that could cut like a knife
She only wanted to be called your highness
She only wanted to take over my life

Chorus (repeated after every second verse):

Josephina, she was meaner
Than any man or woman I have ever known
Guarantee ya if ya see her
Like Medusa she'll reduce ya to a block of stone.

I knew it was a fatal attraction
Just like Oedipus Rex
And she was using Sigmund Freud against me
Mixing everything with sex

That was back in 1972
Maggie Mae was on the radio
When I started to work on Maggie's Farm
But I was catching on too slow

Four years later we found the Lord
And things went from bad to worse
Cause now I was married to a prophetess
With the power to bless and to curse

And man she could curse so that brimstone and fire
Would pour down onto my head
It was Isaiah, Hosea, and Jeremiah
Unless I did as she said

I was a lamb led to the slaughter
I was a sacrificial goat
I was a captive by the rivers of Babylon
Without a paddle, without a boat

For seven years I served her
Then I served her for seven more
I poured all my riches upon her
Just like that Babylonian whore

Then I finally crossed the border
To a place where she couldn't go
It was the land of milk and honey
Even further than Mexico

But when I came back ten years later
She slapped me with the third degree
Hell hath no fury like a woman
When the woman can't let me be.

Chorus

If I Could Turn it Around

If I could turn it around and see the other side
I'm not so innocent it's not so cut and dried
If I could go back and see it from above
I didn't know how to behave, I didn't know how to love

Now the children are grown, there's no going back
I gave what I could give, I'm sorry for the lack
Please don't ask if I'd do it again
I would change some things but that wouldn't change the end

We thought we could change it all
Pride goes before the fall.

I was a spoiled child so full of guile
Give me me an inch and I'd take a mile
I was so full of rage in an angry age
I needed someone to help me wage my endless war.
I was cut down in my prime
But wounds do heal with time.

If I Live Long Enough

Chorus:
If I, if I live long enough
If I live long enough to learn what love is

Love is a little bit like happiness
Chase it and it runs away
Comes upon you when you least expect it
Like manna you collect it day by day

Chorus

Love is a little bit like sacrifice
Gaining what you give away
Complaining sometimes, you're only human
But knowing love will always have its way

Chorus

Love is a lit bit like business
Sometimes you win, sometimes you loses
Sometimes you sign on the dotted line
But first you gotta learn how to choose

Sometimes love is a hunger
Sometimes love is a thirst
But I know our love is stronger
Than even what we had at first

Chorus

Garage Sale Hula

I bought a ukulele in Wailuku
At a rummage sale, bought a radio too
From a roly-poly lady and she sang a song
While her daughter danced the hula and my wife danced along.

The daughter was round and brown as the soil
And my wife has a figure like Olive Oyl
But she sang so pretty and they danced so sweet
Like tellin' a story with their hands and their feet.

It rained every day in Houwelo
On the windward side where the trade winds blow
Livin' off the grid as best we can
Fryin' our bread in a frying pan

I used to be a broker like Paul Gaugin
Till he ran off to Tahiti to be a natural man
But I wanted to go native and I let myself go
On vacation to Hawaii where the coconuts grow

Now I'm just a middle aged Haole* man
Kinda lyin' in the sun tryin' to get a tan
Tryin to learn the ukulele to impress my friends
When I get back to the mainland and the journey ends

No man is an island so the poet did say
That means we're all connected in a deeper way
You can call me bro' when you see me come
We're all God's creatures under the sun.

In the Hawaiian language, the term has been used historically and currently to refer to any foreigner or anything else introduced to the Hawaiian islands of foreign origin.

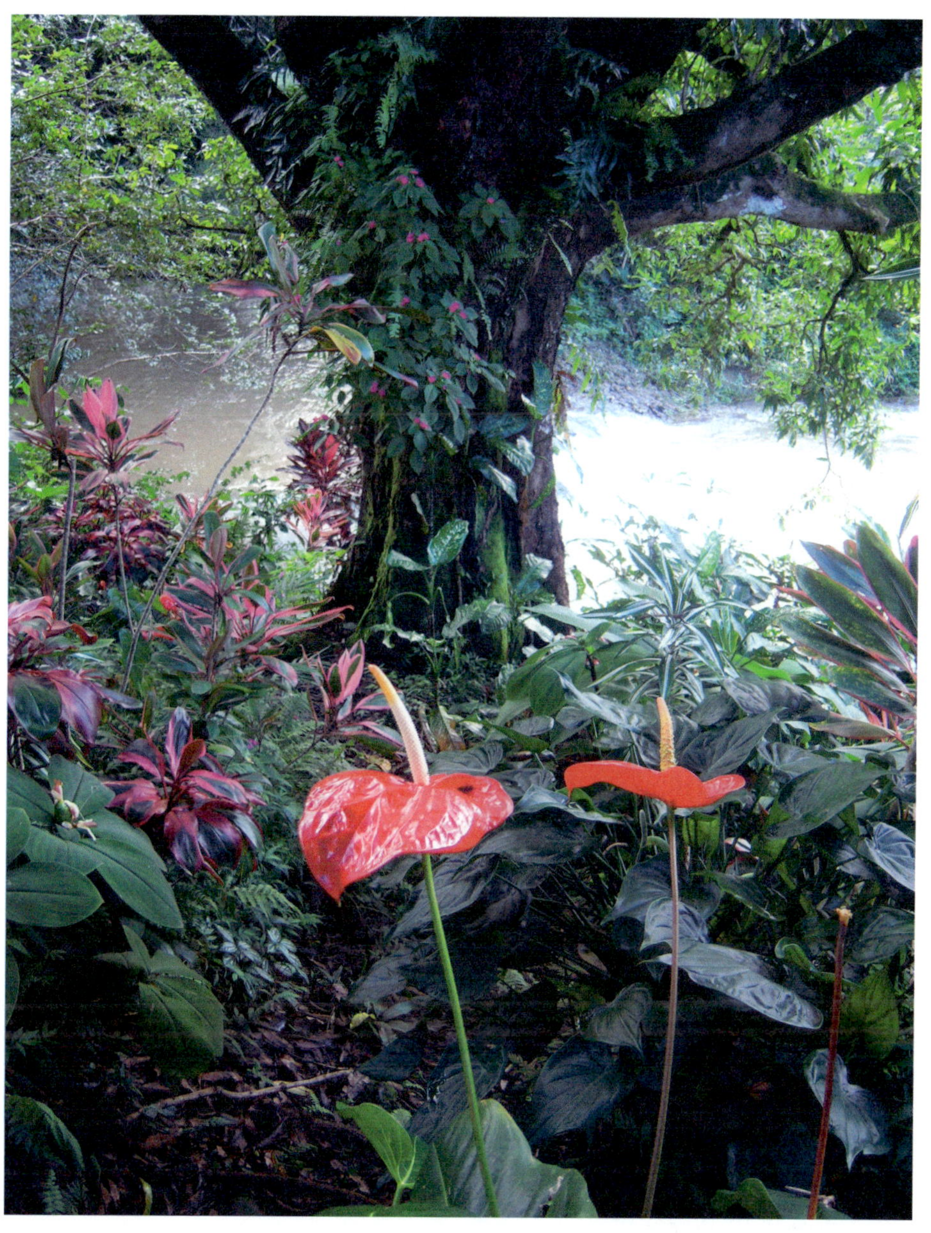

It rained every day in Houwelo
On the windward side where the trade winds blow

55

War in the Family

This ain't Tennessee Williams,
This ain't Eugene O'Neil
Multiply that by a million
Maybe then you'll know how I feel.

War in the family
The plot is thickening
Smiles and deception
It's almost sickening.

It's like Shakespeare or maybe the Bible
Family feuds in a really big way
If you value your survival
Watch your back and mind what you say.

War in the family
The plot is thickening
All the world's a stage
The pulse is quickening.

Starting out with Cain and Abel
What makes us think we're a different breed
Lay lay our cards right on the table
Court's in session, how do you plead.

War in the family
A sword is beckoning
Choosing up sides
For the day of reckoning.

Desdemona loved Othello
What made him think she done him wrong
Shouldn't have smothered her with a pillow
Should have trusted her all along

War in the family
It's so unsettling
Don't get in the middle
You'd just be meddling.

Don't have to tell you about Medea
Her husband left her for a younger bride.
She loved her children she was quite sincere
But still she killed 'em cause he hurt her pride

War in the family
It's so unyielding
Better pay attention
To what your wielding

Absalom may have looked like a hippie
With his hair flowing down his back
He was a prince but he was still pretty creepy
Taking the palace in surprise attack

War in the family
It's not just mythology
Any shrink will tell you
It's only psychology

Ashkelon

Dancing on the sands
Dancing on the shifting sands
Dancing on the ancient sands of Ashkelon.
Dancing with the past
Swaying with the leaves of grass
Nothing ever lasts, but just moves on
Dancing on the ancient sands of Ashkelon.

Planted on the ground
Reaching for the sky all around
Just the gentle sound of the sea.
Kingdoms rise and fall
Does it really matter at all
One more crumbling wall in history.
Dancing with the past, such mystery.

Dancing in the gate
Where once passed the small and the great
Dancing in the gate of Ashkelon.
Soaring like a bird
Dancing to a song without words
Dancing on the potsherds of Ashkelon
Dancing on the potsherds of Ashkelon.

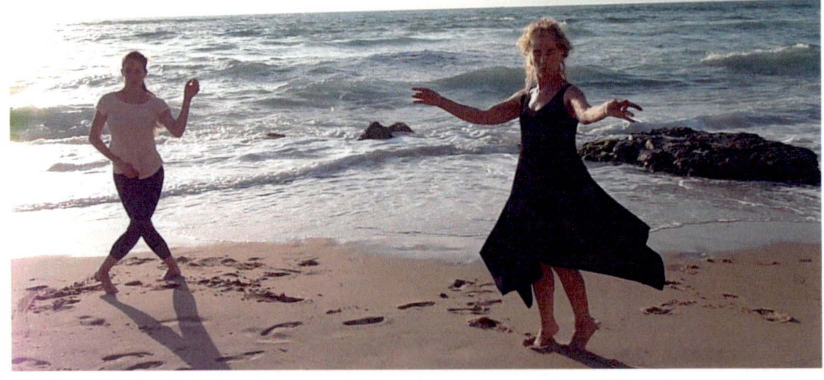

Dancing on the sands of Ashkelon

By the Rivers of Babylon *(paraphrased from Psalm 137)*

By the rivers of Babylon, there we sat down.
By the rivers of Babylon, we sat down and wept
When we remembered Zion,
When we remembered Zion.

There upon the willows our harps were hung
There our captors demanded of us a song.
Sing us a song of Zion
Sing us a song of Zion

How can we sing the Lord's song in a strange land
If I forget thee O Jerusalem, let my right hand
Forget its cunning, forget its skill
Let my tongue cleave to my palate and be forever still.

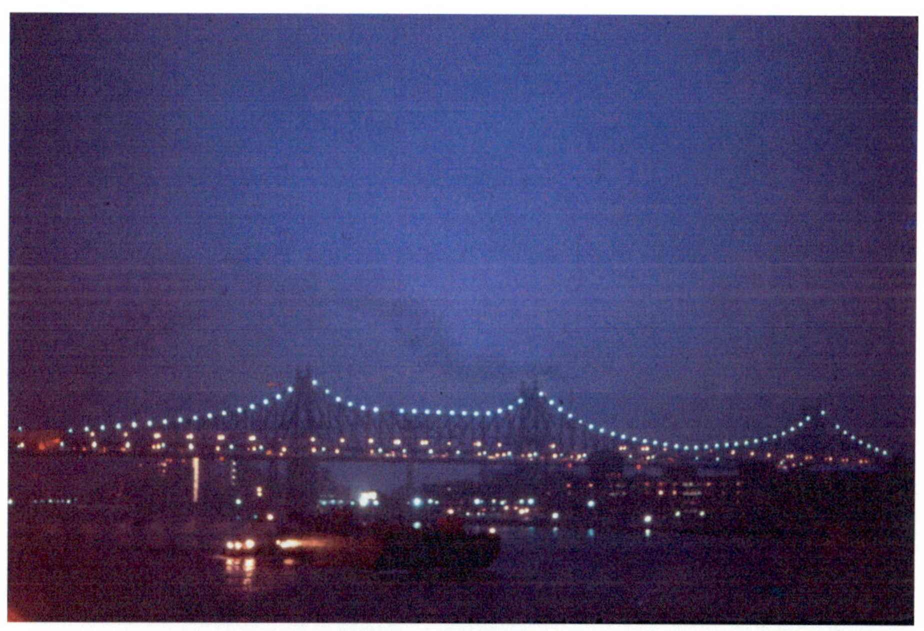

Triborough Bridge, East River, NYC (1975)

The Train Song

I can't explain it's like I'm on a train, I see the fields go by.
I close my eyes it's like I'm hypnotized, I fall asleep for a while.
Train is rocking and my dreams unlocking all my memories
Shifting places and I'm seeing faces from my history

Time just gets swifter and I'm just a drifter
A comet approaching the sun
My orbit grows small as I fall and I fall
And the years just rush by one by one.

Can't stop your brain and you can't stop the train
    and you can't stop time
Life is sweet but the days are fleet, it's part of the design
Please be patient till we reach the station as we surely shall.
Enjoy the ride watch the countryside, that's the rationale.

And then it goes back and it's hard to keep track
Of where I was when I began
I am him inside and I cannot divide
The child that is father to man.

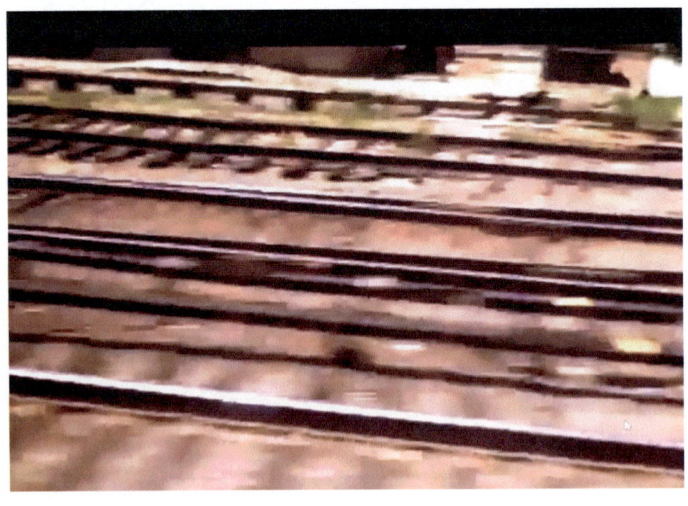

Amtrak Hudson Line *(stroboscopic effect reverses perceived direction of motion)*

These Three Things

*"There be three things which are too wonderful for me, yea, four which I
know not: The way of an eagle in the air; the way of a serpent upon a rock;
the way of a ship in the midst of the sea; and the way of a man with a maid."*
—   *Proverbs 30:18-19*

Chorus:
These three things are too wonderful for me
Four too marvelous to say
I stand and wonder at the beauty of it all
It takes my breath away

The way of an eagle mounting up to the sky
Riding the currents in the air.
Spreading its wings as it soars so high
Dancing and spinning in a pair.

Chorus

The way of a serpent sunning on a rock it lies
Its name is painted on its skin
Twisting and writhing as it stalks its prize
Tell me where is the sin

Chorus

The way of a ship in the midst of the sea
Riding on the swell
On the back of an elephant like a tiny little flea
In our hearts we wish them well

Chorus

The way of a young man and the woman of his desire
Choosing to share their lives
Gives me the hope that the world will not expire
As long as this love survives

61

Art in the Public Realm

Essays

Between Decadence and Renaissance (1999)

I have been interested in trends ever since I worked on Wall Street. Well, not actually Wall Street, but two blocks over on Water Street and prior to that in midtown Manhattan, for two firms which underwent forced sales at bargain basement prices after they jumped on the wrong bandwagon. That bandwagon got started in the 1970's, when foreign currencies, treasury bonds, and stock market indexes began trading on futures exchanges along with wheat, corn, and pork bellies. The failure to either gauge or respond appropriately to the discrepancy between the actual, physical or real, and the representation, symbol or virtual led to the mortgage crisis and crash of 2008. This is an essay on art, where symbols began on the walls of caves. The difference is that they knew that the actual horned beast could kill you.

I believe that all trends, whether economic or aesthetic, are cyclical. Artistic styles have fluctuated between realism and abstraction throughout history. Realism mimics our eye-brain perception by utilizing the laws of perspective as the Renaissance artists rediscovered from the Greeks. Abstraction is flat, iconographic, and appeals to those who have been initiated and can interpret the code. Byzantine icons, according to the monks who still make them, are written, not painted. They lack perspective. Abstract expressionism as well as pop art and graffiti art are also iconographic, requiring a clergy of art critics to uphold it. Mid-century critics made a fetish of the flatness of a painting.

Another alternating trend, that operates independently of the one just described is Romanticism and Classicism. These trends constantly repeat and renew themselves cyclically. The Classical muse returned in the Renaissance and again in the Enlightenment, and once again in the Neo-Classical movements in both Europe and America in the late 19th century. Classicism favors perspective, straight lines and regular shapes, and is international in spirit, not regional or parochial. The other pole is Romanticism, which arose in Germany and England in the late 18th and early 19th centuries. Romanticism harked back to the Middle Ages and the chivalric tradition, and also included Orientalism which began, perhaps with the Crusades, the first European encounter with the Middle East. Romanticism favors natural, irregular forms and is regional and parochial, often national in spirit.

Sometimes, of course there is an overlap. As I learned on Wall Street, there is no perfect formula. These cycles are difficult to identify, except in retrospect, and correlations between different cycles are even more difficult to verify or to explain, like wheels within wheels. For example, some people believe in a correlation between rising or falling hemlines and stock prices.

There is a third eternal cycle which occurs in art, politics, religion, and in fact in every field of human endeavor. Periods of decadence and renaissance fluctuate throughout history. Every renaissance, every reformation, every revolution, every revival contains the seeds of its own decadence. Late Roman revivals of classic Greek sculpture and architecture were wrought through a preponderance of technical ability but a diminution of simplicity, originality, and depth.

I am using the terms "decadence" and "renaissance" in their most literal sense. By decadence I do not mean simply a decline in moral values; I mean more a fixation on death and decay as opposed to birth and rebirth. Like in the late Roman Empire, societies in the decadent phase experience a low birth rate, but enjoy indoor plumbing and free sexual expression without the need or expectation of procreation, especially among the upper class. This is a natural reaction to the stagnation and hypocrisy that befalls all reformations, revivals, revolutions, and counter-revolutions sooner or later as they become institutionalized.

In 1999 the Mayor of New York threatened to shut down the Brooklyn Museum for exhibiting a mixed media depiction of the Virgin Mary in which one of the materials was elephant dung. (The painting sold at auction sixteen years later for 4.6 million dollars.) Is excrement the last taboo or, as some, including then New York mayor Rudy Guilliani, may see it, is it blasphemy? However, both scatology and blasphemy are old hat. Marcel Duchamp reputedly entered the urinal into an non-juried exhibition held by the Society of Independent Artists in New York in 1917. It was refused, which did not prevent Duchamp from capitalizing on its notoriety for the rest of his life. There are those, including myself, who believe that the piece, signed by the fictitious R Mutt,was actually submitted by the Baroness Elsa von Freytag-Loringhoven. Duchamp indicated in a letter to his sister Suzanne, written in 1917, that a female friend of his had sent him the urinal for submission. The Baroness was an early member of the Dada movement, which was itself a reaction to the decadence that caused World War I, which resulted in the end of the Austrian Empire, the Ottoman Empire, the British Empire, and the Russian Empire.

Another contributor to the Brooklyn Museum exhibit was Damien Hirst, who displayed an eviscerated cow's head, complete with maggots, in a plexiglass cube. "High Art" is fixated on death, decay and defecation. Excretion follows copious consumption. Bigger and more lavish bathrooms are always a sign of decadence as the fruits of technology and empire are disseminated ever more rapidly, and unevenly. I do not say that something is excretive in the pejorative sense, simpy descriptive, and yet I   must observe that whenever shit or rotting flesh are put on display, the scent has been removed. Ubiquitous deodorizing or perfuming is another hallmark of a society in decadence. In losing the distinction between the symbol and the referent, one might adopt the false conclusion   that it ain't shit if it don't smell like shit.

Concurrent with Brooklyn Museum exhibit the country was fixated on the President's semen stain on a red dress. This revelation, which led to impeachment, was preceded by a years long prologue, exposition, and denouement on television - voyeurism reminiscent of soap opera. But the dissemination of this scandal did not serve a strictly prurient interest. It was a public pillorying. Also in art, there are two simultaneous trends, one prurient, relying on shock value, and the other moralizing, preachy, pedantic. This combination is not unusual, in fact quite common. In the late, or decadent stage of the Dutch still life genre in the 1600's, the table was practically collapsing under the weight of all of all the fruit, game, flowers, silver service, and other affirmations of prosperity, yet still the glass of wine perched at the edge of the table, sometimes even caught in mid-air indicated the precariousness life. A skull placed in the composition became known as memento mori, literally, "remember that you must die."

The Decadent Movement was a late 19th century artistic and literary movement in Europe. Charles Baudelaire, Oscar Wilde, Aubrey Beardsley, and Edvard Munch are among the best known participants in the movement which combined eroticism with morbidity, flouted social conventions and was often involved with the occult, sometimes Satan worship. Decadence was associated with cultural decline, particularly the decline of the Roman Empire. Fin de siècle in Europe was a time of great uncertainty and pessimism. It is not unusual in transitional times to contemplate the decline of empire or culture. The Decadence Movement was a transition between Romanticism and Modernism.

A follow-up to the Brooklyn Museum's exhibit was an exhibit at the Whitney Museum in NY. The installation included garbage cans, the sound of marching jack boots, and quotations from demonized politicians, such as Mayor Giuliani (who attempted to close the Brooklyn Museum) displayed in the typography preferred by the Nazi party. One of the Whitney heiresses withdrew all support for the museum which bears her name. The producer of that installation learned well from those he emulated, though with a sense of irony. The Nazis raised propaganda to an art form through their use of "installations" and political theater such as Kristallnacht, the Night of Broken Glass. I heard an interview once in which Dada was characterized as the artistic herald of the systematized absurdity and perversity which brought about, in its final political expression, perfectly efficient factories of death. Perhaps this is why others have said that there can be no art after the Holocaust.

For these installations, attendance is not required. Their real art form is publicity. The "fifteen minutes of fame" has become the end which justifies the means. They subvert and sever the connection between art and beauty, art and artifact, art and pilgrimage, art and eternity, art and taste and become what art was in Communist Russia or Nazi Germany, that is politics. It is political not in the larger sense of the commonweal or public works which gave rise to the treasury of art produced through the Farm Security Administration of the 1930's. It is political in the form of identity politics. When art is severed from taste, it is removed from seeking a connection to the individual viewer, for it is the individual who is, in the end, the only arbiter of his or her taste, for better or worse.

It is interesting to note the fact that some of the major political operators recent times, namely dictators, have fashioned themselves artists. Hitler was a painter and a frustrated architect who collaborated closely with Albert Speer, imposing his own meglomaniacal taste on projects. Generalissimo Franco was a better than an amateur painter. Mao immersed himself in Chinese classical literature and wrote poetry in the classical style. Stalin, according to historian Simon Seba Montefiore, micromanaged the Soviet theater and film industry and even wrote lyrics for Russian musicals such as this one, which Montefiore has translated in his book, *Stalin: The Court of the Red Tsar*:

> "A joyful song is easy for the heart.
> It doesn't bore you ever.
> And all the villages small and big
> Adore the song;
> Big towns love the tune."

Saddam Hussein wrote a novel, *Zabiba and the King*, which was produced as a musical in Baghdad. It begins: "What is more wondrous and delightful than heroines and the level of great deeds, and even miracles in Iraq!"

Dictators' tastes may run to the reactionary, but it shows that art is not necessarily ennobling. Just as artists are sovereign in their own world (as it says in the Bible, the pot does not talk back to the potter) dictators impose themselves on a bigger canvas, the canvas of State.

On a visit to NY, I visited a prestigious gallery in Soho. In the main exhibit space was a pile of PVC pipe elbows such as one finds attached to, of course, a toilet. I thought to myself, who would possibly have such a thing in their home? Obviously the gallery, which pays high rent, expects to sell it. Then I consulted a reference guide to NY galleries and discovered that this gallery sells primarily to museums and corporations. The intended purchase is decided by a committee, or a fiduciary chosen by committee. No one has to like it. If the gallery puts its imprimatur on it, perhaps causes some of the artist's works to be accepted on donation by a museum or two, the value begins to escalate through a form of manipulated demand. This too is politics. If I may coin a phrase, I would call it Corporate Socialism. Art, the ultimate one-of-a-kind is the last asset to become a commodity, transaction driven, just like the stock or futures market.

In finance there is a process called "disintermediation" when the public invests directly in government bonds as opposed to doing so with through the intermediation of a bank. In art, the market is highly intermediated by experts. In an interview in "talk" magazine (April 2000, p. 184), Mary Brennan, the mother of Damien Hirst, the installation artist famous for his eviscerated animals, quoted her son as saying: "I love art but I don't like the art world; I'm gonna play 'em at their own game and then I can do what I want to do."

Regarding the "art world," who does like 'em? The Norwegian artist, Odd Nerdrum, decided not to play the game and published an essay in the form of a paid advertisement in *ARTnews* (Oct. 1999). Summing up the contemporary art world, he writes: "For many hundreds of years, craftsmanship was also a part of the concept of "Art." This is no longer the case. Only ideas count. And the predominant art world has been brutally uniform, either you go along or you are out... Critics and curators have been brought up into a stern clergy. The question is not whether a work is well done, but if it carries the right ideas. Preferably it should be poorly done, in order for the true message to reach through, just like in the Middle Ages."

This stern clergy harshly discourages the conflation of truth and beauty (Keats' eternal dyad), forbidding their vernacular expression and instead promoting a rigid, self-serving and self-referential system. Visual and artistic literacy is not widely taught or disseminated. The public is alienated from "high end" art. This dichotomy did not always exist, nor does it exist per force in all countries. No wonder the people dwell in darkness with sentimental trinkets and pastiches on their shelves and walls, while the "priests" solicit contributions to cultural institutions like indulgences. Art has become the secular religion, and it is a highly orthodox one at that. Deconstructionism is the philosophical handmaiden of that orthodoxy, providing a context, a motive, a world view, a lens to flatten the world and make it coincide with whatever we currently believe. The expectation, as Oscar Wilde wrote, is that "life imitates art far more than art imitates life." In other words, art will save us from ourselves. Like, Wagner, that paragon of late Romanticism when it became decadent, they expect art to assume the functions of religion.

I do not know if it is possible to transcend the age we are born into. Irony, despair, and anti-authoritarianism are legitimate responses to some of the phenomena of this age, but when they become highly stylized and mannered, as they have indeed become, then it is time for artists to search their souls and become, once again Renaissance people, reconciling the spiritual and the natural, the public and the personal realms, and creating beauty in the bargain.

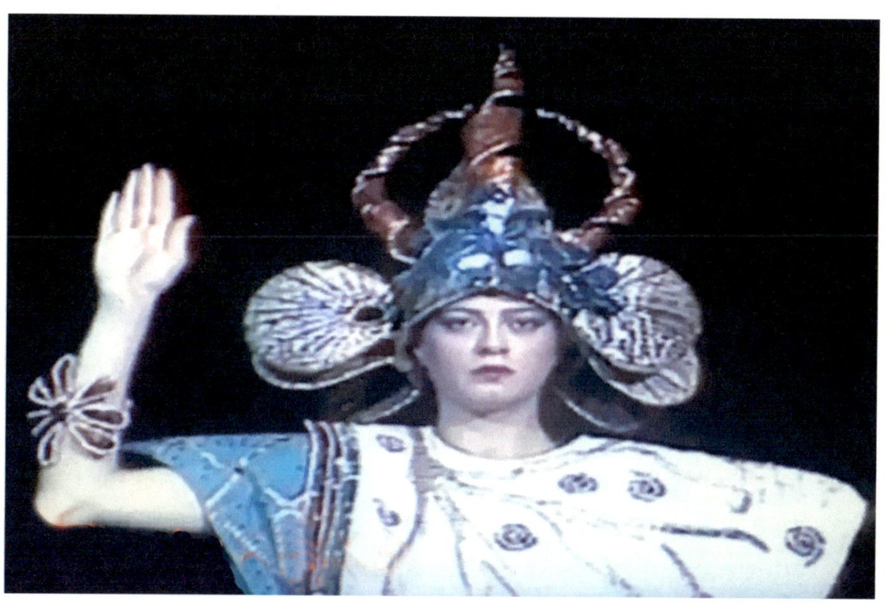

Zabiba from the Baghdad production of *"Zabiba and the King"*

Why You Hate Art - You know you do

Americans, the vast majority, are not merely indifferent to art; they have an antipathy to it for various reasons. This essay will attempt to chronicle nine of those reasons:

I

Dada, which evolved into post-modernism, has been described as anti-art, and quite aptly. All movements in the past have challenged conventions, but Dada and its post-modern progeny have challenged what have been the defining characteristics of art for tens of thousands of years: originality, agency, artifact, selectivity, craftsmanship, and beauty. Regardless of who submitted the famous urinal, it was not only not made by that person, it was a mass-produced item. Even the anonymous artists of the past exhibited agency and craftsmanship. Admittedly, it is difficult to kill all the birds with one stone. "Fountain" can still be seen as beautiful, even more beautiful than a gargoyle. Andy Warhol's five hour and twenty minute film, "Sleep," a single shot which showed his friend sleeping, took aim at the notion of selectivity. He himself defined it as an "anti-film." Robert Rauschenberg's smudged, blank sheet of paper entitled "Drawing," which he attested was an erasure of a drawing by Willem de Kooning, is considered a landmark in post-modern art. It attacked the notions of originality, artifact, beauty, agency, craftsmanship, and selectivity, effectively killing all the birds with one stone.

Before discussing the other reasons why many Americans are not merely indifferent to contemporary art, but have an antipathy to it, I would submit that reason number one is that they feel they are either being preached to or lied to or made fun of. The other nine reasons puts the shoe on the other foot.

II

Culture is an agglomeration. Although only the top layer is most visible, ideas, even abandoned ones, are built one on top of another. To begin at the beginning, the Puritan fathers distrusted not only art, but also all adornment. "Charm is deceptive and beauty is vain," as Proverbs 31:30 has it. Even the singing of hymns was banned. They did not allow instruments in their churches, rather, music was restricted the singing of Psalms in unison. The organ and the singing of hymns did not enter the Protestant churches in America until the 19th century. This fear of idolatry can be found in other pietistic religious sects, even to this day.

Paradoxically, even as some worldly attractions were shunned, and pleasure itself mistrusted, the idea of material prosperity as a sign of God's favor is part of this same Puritan heritage. The Puritans were Calvinists, who, in the dichotomy of predestination vs. choice, strongly favored a theology of predestination. To them, material prosperity was a sign of God's blessing. As Jonathan Edwards, the evangelist whose preaching helped inaugurate the revival known as the Great Awakening, wrote in his book Charity and Its Fruits (1738), "But if you place your happiness in God, in glorifying Him and in serving Him by doing good, in this way above all others you will promote your wealth and honor and pleasure here below, and obtain hereafter a crown of ... glory and pleasure forevermore at God's right hand." Prosperity could be both a sign of Divine favor and a channel of blessing, but not a conduit for the ostentatious display of wealth and power such as characterized the estates, the castles and the churches of Europe. The purchase or commissioning of art would have seemed immodest if not idolatrous to the Puritan mind.

From the middle of the nineteenth century, a new philosophy conquered America, again from England. This was called "Utilitarianism." It was first promulgated by Jeremy Bentham. The Oxford English Dictionary defines a Utilitarian as "one who considers utility the standard of whatever is good for man." Utility then, according to Bentham, is the property in a thing "whereby it tends to produce benefit, advantage, pleasure, good, or happiness (all this in the present case comes to the same thing)." He later added the words "profit, convenience, and emolument" (remuneration).

The problem is that words, such as "pleasure, " may mean something completely different to different people at different times. Bentham was a Materialist who regarded anything which could not be measured as illusory. Thus he repudiated any kind of spiritual pleasure such as that afforded by art or music. Nothing was inherently a source of pleasure, and therefore good; it was only so in that it provided some profit or convenience or opportunity for such. As his successor, William Stanley Jevons, so succinctly put it, "Value depends entirely on utility." It was the perfect philosophy for the Industrial Revolution."Yankee practicality" is still admired, which is why so many who have been materially prospered would think nothing of spending lavishly on their home or purchasing a boat or a snowmobile, or even a second snowmobile. It is perceived as practical, ingenious, utilitarian, whereas a work of art is not.

The 2002 Nobel Prize for economics was shared by an Israeli psychologist, Daniel Kahneman. His startling breakthrough: Money can't buy happiness. Finally, a scientific negation of Utilitarianism. In other words, with all the quantification of goods and services, the question remains, what is the amount of happiness that it brings? The conclusion: once subsistence is achieved an the basic necessities are covered, no amount of money will make you happier. Some experiments also reveal an anomaly in human nature. The vast majority of people do not make decisions based on a clear assessment of risk versus reward (pleasure vs. pain). They are far more risk averse, much more afraid of losing what they have than desirous of gaining more. And why shouldn't they be, when we now know that once a certain threshold is passed, that no amount more will increase happiness. Yet many of the most successful have taken more risk and have courted and encountered failure. The Constitution does not vouchsafe happiness for us, only the right to pursue it. I might add that it is the minority, the risk takers who purchase and invest in art. Later we will see how anti-elitism and resentment in the face of the astronomical increase in value of these assets has added to the public's distrust of high end art.

IV

It is my theory that a nation's capacity for art appreciation is closely tied to its capacity for meditation. It is not even necessary that the majority practice a form of meditation, just that there is an element of society which does, and that this meditative group is seen as part of the fabric of society. This is certainly the case in Asian cultures, such as Japan with its practitioners of Zen Buddhism. The tea ceremony is the cultivated practice of appreciating the tea, the teacup, the tea-house, and the ceremony itself in all of their aspects.

China had its tradition of court officials retiring or going into exile in seclusion to practice painting, poetry, and calligraphy. In France, what I might call the Gross Domestic Product of Meditation is spread more evenly among the public. Each region, for example, produces its own distinctive wine or cheese based on its own particular climate and soil. The subtle character of such a wine or such a cheese requires sufficient time not only to produce it, but also to enjoy it. As time is allocated for a long, leisurely meal, taste becomes refined, and this refinement is transmitted through the culture. Taste itself becomes meditation.

Throughout Europe, playwrights such as Vaslav Havel and writers such as Andre Malraux have shuttled from the arts and letters to government and back and not merely to write their memoirs. Plato's idea of the philosopher king is still alive. I believe that this connection between the gross national output of meditation and the net appreciation of art has to do with the perception and definition of time, which is culturally based. The culture which values time more than possessions will take the time to fall in love with a work of art, and not a mere infatuation.

European and Asian appreciation of their own cultural artifacts is widespread in their societies. For example, on a popular game show for many years in Iran, two opponents face off and recite couplets from classical Persian poetry. Each couplet must begin with the last letter of the previously recited couplet. Even first graders compete. We have made a virtue out of busyness. A whole new genre of television drama, taking place in the hospital, or law office, or the White House, ennobles characters who only have time to carry on a dialogue on the run, in the corridor, and who have no time for any meaningful personal relationship outside of their work. Cut to the commercial which shows a soccer mom in the driver's seat, hastily accepting a microwaved, pre-packaged cup of soup handed to her like a baton in a relay race through the window of her car.

There was one exception, one movement that arose as a reaction against Utilitarianism. Emerson, one of the leading lights of the Transcendental Movement, wrote that Utilitarianism was a "stinking philosophy." He, along with Thoreau and Emily Dickinson constituted a small group "marching to a different drummer," as Thoreau put it. Transcendentalism represented a backlash in the country which gave rise to some of our great poetry, essays, and art. The Hudson River School of painting engendered the whole idea of American landscape and gave rise to our National Park system.

V

The valuing of possessions or things instead of time both destroys the environment and devalues art. Religious asceticism, which devalues this world in comparison to the world to come also devalues art. Even Plato, the arch-idealist held art in low esteem. The twentieth century gave rise to new forms of both tendencies. On the materialist side, the mass-media, first in print, then though radio and television, gave rise to commercialism, advertising and its twin, consumerism. Mass-production began with Henry Ford's pithy statement that "they can have any color they want, as long as it's black," and has taken off toward more and more customization. In a "public service" announcement, the Advertising Council equates greater freedom with more choices, more products made possible through more information presented to us by our friendly advertiser. As psychological tests have shown however, an over-abundance of choices results in paralysis and dissatisfaction with our ultimate choices.

Flashy, glossy, or slick techniques in speech or imagery that is used to persuade the masses to political or commercial ends is a form of demagoguery. Leni Riefenstahl, Hitler's propagandist film-maker, used columns of light projected into the night sky to dramatize the Nuremburg rally when she filmed it. This awe inspiring effect was used seventy years later at Ground Zero to accentuate our national loss of the Twin Towers and the many lives that were destroyed with it. (This is discussed further in my essay "The Evolution of Propaganda.")

American democracy was originally conceived as a system to bring order and contentment to a society of independent farmers and yeomen (craftsmen-proprietors). Production was decentralized and distribution was localized at the market or the trade fair. Little by little the situation reversed as production became centralized and consolidated and distribution beat a path to every door first through the Sears Roebuck Catalog, and more recently through the internet and the proliferation of big box stores in every available commercial zone. Today, the artist-crafts-person is one of the last vestiges of the independent yeoman, flying in the face of the modern market-driven economy.

VI

Consumerism has penetrated every aspect of our lives. Politics, religion, entertainment, and even mating are largely driven by market analysis. Consumerism panders and flatters the public into a suspension of disbelief. Marshall Fields, which opened in Chicago in 1887, is often credited with being the first modern department store. It was designed by the architect, Henry Hobson Richardson, whose ornate style is known as Richardsonian Romanesque. The idea was that any woman entering from the crowded and dirty street would feel that she had entered the Palace of Versailles. And she would be treated as royalty.

The mass-produced and mass-marketed product, whether it be an article of clothing with a designer label, a cruise, a food or beverage, a piece of furniture, or an image is perceived as "just as good" as an original, fresh creation. "Just as good as home baked," as they say. In the extreme, many Americans even prefer the facsimile to the authentic. Mass-production smooths out the rough spots and introduces a comforting predictability. Furthermore, a mass-produced item has a value which is easy to quantify either by the purchaser or by anyone seeing it in a neighbor's home or driveway. Art, on the other hand, was once defined by its uniqueness in the world, that is until it merged with "popular art" in the consumer age.

In *The Decline of Pleasure* by Walter Kerr, a renowned theater critic of the mid-twentieth century. (first published in 1962 by Simon and Schuster) he wrote: "In a way, I find it as easy to forgive kitsch as I do a baby for drooling. Given our convictions, how better might the popular arts behave? Our deepest beliefs in the twentieth century command us to dismiss the arts, popular or otherwise: they have not had value, they do not have value, they will not have value."

In the fifty plus years since this was written, Consumerism has succeeded, as the Advertising Council promised, in making more and better educated consumers out of us. Not only have production values continued to improve, but originality, honesty, and depth in the popular arts, first in music, then film, and finally television, have waxed, though sometimes also waned. On the whole I would say, the quality of the popular arts has improved from the early 1960's. Looking at a broadcast of Cecil B. DeMille's "The Ten Commandments," a lot of it seems like a lavish high school pageant. The acting is more theatrical than cinematic.

Some critics claim there is no difference between the popular and the fine arts, between low brow and high brow. Igor Stravinsky delivered a series of lectures at Harvard between 1939 and 1940. In one of them he made a brief parenthetical statement which I have not forgotten: "All art is based on aristocratic culture." I don't think he meant that all art was inspired by aristocratic sources, or that all artists are aristocrats. I think he was talking about the type of cultural transaction that takes place between artist and society. Despite the shrinking of the Middle Class, which has been taking place over the last half a century, Americans do not like the idea of an aristocracy. We are inculcated from a young age to associate connoisseurship with an indolent leisure class.

On the subject of class and art, I recently heard of the work of Ruby K. Payne, author of *Bridges out of Poverty*. She observes that there is a code for each social class: upper, middle, and lower. In order to enter another class one must learn the code. For example, in eating, the lower class values quantity, the middle class quality, and the upper class presentation. In collecting, an area which directly impacts art, the lower class collects people. That is one of the reasons why it is sometimes seen as an act of disloyalty to break out. The middle class collects things, especially things that have a discreet and ascertainable value. I refer back to the philosophy of Utilitarianism, according to which happiness must be defined through the attainment of material things to which value can be ascribed. Finally, the upper class collects unique objects and experiences. The middle class does not have the code, that is, the training, the experience, or the inclination to deal with one-of-a-kind. There would be no way to compare its value or worth so it can be justified to others, one's spouse, one's friends and neighbors. The middle class, that is, the bourgeoisie, require not only quality, but its commercial validation.

In his essay, "Distinction: A Social Critique of the Judgment of Taste" (published originally in French in 1979 based on research conducted in the sixties), the French sociologist, Pierre Bourdieu discusses how art is an important component of the code which separates the classes. "A work of art has meaning and interest only for someone who possesses the cultural competence, that is, the code, into which it is encoded. The conscious or unconscious implementation of explicit or implicit schemes of perception and appreciation which constitutes pictorial or musical culture is the hidden condition for recognizing the styles characteristic of a period, a school or an author, and, more generally, for the familiarity with the internal logic of works that aesthetic enjoyment presupposes. A beholder who lacks the specific code feels lost in a chaos of sounds and rhythms, colours and lines, without rhyme or reason."

This recognition of the subtext of a work of art is like face recognition, not entirely conscious. Even the experts who identify skillful forgeries must rely partly on intuition. The appreciation of art is not a purely academic exercise which can be taught. It is also a function of familiarity, sometimes the result of the exposure of multiple generations. This flies in the face of the American ethos of the "self-made man." Among its other functions, art is a conversation, not only with the contemporaneous public, but also with history, including art history. In literature this is called "allusion." The writer is conversing not only with the reader, but with other writers past or present. The more we lose our sense and knowledge of art history, the shallower our art becomes. When the Russians launched Sputnik, we asked ourselves, how far behind are we? The result was an improvement in the science curriculum.

The quality and appreciation of art is not a zero sum game, like Mercantilism, the belief that wealth consisted ultimately in gold and silver, and that since these metals were finite in supply, one nation was bound to prosper only at the expense of another. This idea may have caused a lot of wars, but, after all, something had to be done with all that gold. Spanish palaces competed with cathedrals to gild the lily. Spain, in turn, competed with France and England, and a lot of a art was produced. Instead art is the ultimate affirmation that wealth can indeed be created, not merely extracted.

In the Age of Mercantilism, the wealth was accrued by the state and the church. Today there is a consolidation of power and wealth, an accelerating trend allowing the purveyors of consumables, namely corporate managers and major shareholders to accrue valuables such as major artworks. However, unlike the past, when the public felt itself a participant through king or clergy. Many artworks, from ancient Roman antiquities to over a thousand Picassos, join a multitude of untold treasures locked up in just one storage facility among many in Switzerland. This treatment of art as a commodity has elicited criticism from many art patrons and collectors.

It must be said that museums are doing an excellent job in attracting and educating the public. However, according to a survey published by the National Endowment for the Arts, attendance at arts events such as opera, jazz, classical music, ballet, musical theater, plays, art museum and gallery visits, has dropped over the past two decades to about one third of all adults.

VII

An adjunct of consumerism deserves its own category. In 1899, Thorstein Veblen, an American economist and sociologist, coined the term "conspicuous consumption" in his book, *The Theory of the Leisure Class*. In the past thirty years, since the failure of "trickle down economics" to indeed trickle down, America has very much come to resemble the age of the Robber Barons which Veblen studied. The acquisitiveness of these captains of industry has already been noted. As Adam Davidson points out in an article in the New York Times (May 30, 2012) titled "How the Art Market Thrives on Inequality, art is not a commodity. Because each piece of fine art is unique and can't be owned by anybody else, it does a more powerful and subtle job of signaling wealth than virtually any other luxury good. High prices are, quite literally, central to the signal. You don't spend $120 million to show that you're a savvy investor who's hoping to flip a Munch for $130 million. You're spending $120 million, in part, to show that you can blow $120 million on something that can't possibly be worth that much in any marketplace." This type of thinking is not only foreign, but antithetical to the logic of the average American. But if we take the economics to the next iteration, following these "priceless" works of art beyond the lifespan of the collector, we find that many of these works are donated to museums to be enjoyed by the public. Inheritance tax law makes it almost impossible to pass down a complete collection intact.

Thus, we find that art straddles two completely different economies, the commodity economy and the gift economy. These two economies have always coexisted, as Lewis Hyde points out in his book, *The Gift, Creativity and the Artist in the Modern World* (originally subtitled in the hardcover edition, Imagination and the Erotic Life of Property. Random House 1983). The purchase and sale of a commodity is an arms length transaction which depends on an objective valuation and does not depend upon or engender relationship. The exchange of a gift, whether taking place among Pacific Northwest Coast Indians in a Potltach (from which we get our word "potluck") or South Sea Islanders, or through grants, fellowships, scholarships and other gifts in modern society, does create and sustain relationship.

Both forms of exchange are well accepted in our society. The problem arises when they become confused. We have already touched upon the effects of advertising in our day and age, but perhaps the most pernicious is how it presents a commodity transaction as if it were a gift exchange. This has become even more insidious with the increased personalization of marketing made possible by new technologies. Commercial interests ask us to become their "friend" on social networks. Employees are referred to as "partners."

I once asked a poet at a book fair, how's business? He replied, "Poetry is a gift, not a business." The survival of the artist is a balancing act between the gift and the commodity economies. Many people have the designation, "Organ Donor" on their driver's license. Though it sometimes occurs, selling organs is considered inappropriate because they belong in the gift economy. Art has always straddled these two economies, and this seeming ambivalence has contributed perhaps to the public's ambivalence toward art.

VIII

The next reason that art is despised is that it has become the secular religion in modern society. Once again the root cause is a philosophy, and once again, it is a philosophy not indigenous to America, but one that has been adopted. In April of 2000, I read a piece, a manifesto that ran as a paid advertisement in ArtNews. Odd Nerdrum, a Norwegian realist, or surrealist painter, declared himself not an artist but a kitsch maker. Modern art, he wrote was indebted to the philosopher Immanuel Kant who suggested that art existed in the realm of intellectual judgments and not in the realm of sensuous appeal. Since then art has been more concerned with the purity of thought than with the sensuousness of the body. This purity of thought has become the correctness of thinking. In other words, art has become politics. Nerdrum, who uses techniques of the Old Masters to portray human flesh and expression, had been ignored, even chastised by the art establishment for many years. Now, he understood where he really belonged. Along with several other artists he published *On Kitsch, a Manifesto.*

Of course Kant was not the first philosopher to distrust art that is created or enjoyed purely for pleasure. Plato, one of the earliest and most influential philosophers, relegated art to mere mimesis, at three removes from his "ideal" and thus inferior to both philosophy and poetry. In his book, The Painted Word, author Tom Wolfe describes the migration of art education from the art school and studio apprenticeship to the university, where, in order to justify itself as an academic subject, art became, "as literary, as academic, as mannered, as clubby, as the salon painting against which it first rebelled." By literary, he means that it needs to be explained or justified with words, preferably big words. Like religion as described by a theologian, it can seem pretty dry.

Along with this migration of art toward the purely intellectual, the role of the curator has become dominant. In his book, *Curationism: How Curating Took Over the Art World and Everything Else* (Pluto Press 2015) David Balzer explains how the role of the curator has expanded from a catetaker of objects to the dominant force in selecting, editing, and labeling everything from food to art. As a result, our everyday lives become a curated experience, and it is only through curating that the importance and value of an object or experience can be transmitted.

IX

The last reason I will touch upon is the present trend toward a form of populism that mistakes equality for equivalence. In the pursuit of equal opportunity, excellence and mediocrity are given the same due, like the children's soccer league which handed out a trophy to every participant. By the same token, self help books declare everyone to be an artist. It is definitely beneficial for everybody to learn art, in its history, theory and practice. But just because we can all read doesn't make us all writers.

I spoke to a former artist who now runs a gallery which includes a sculpture garden. I asked her if she was doing any art and she replied that she was too busy with the gallery. I guess it's one or the other, I responded, though I realized that there have been exceptions like Alfred Stieglitz or even the composer Charles Ives, who sold insurance by day. I told her that my mother made only six stone sculptures in her life but that were so well done that an appraiser from Sothebys thought they were made by Jean Arp. Was she or was she not an artist? I asked.

Perhaps I have revealed my opinion by referring to the gallery owner as a "former" artist. The question of what is an artist is complex and depends to some degree on time and culture. The Latin "artifex" from which the English word is derived means artificer, artist, craftsman, workman, worker, or artisan, showing that there was no division between art and craft but a clear division between art and nature. The word for artist in Hebrew shares the same root as the word for training or practice. In other words, an artist is one who practices art. In this, the artist is similar to a shoemaker. However, the shoemaker must produce to the taste of the market. There is no history of avant-garde shoemakers. In this respect art is not merely a living, it's a life.

"Yes. I believe she was an artist," the gallery owner replied. I wanted to believe this, despite the fact that a studio she had put together on her property had never been used. I believed that if an archaeologist were to find one of her pieces in a thousand years, he or she would validate her artistry and thus, her as an artist. Perhaps some of the ambivalence or antipathy toward art stems from the uncertainty of what an artist is.

Instead of addressing that question directly, which is beyond the scope of this essay, I will address it obliquely. The traits that are necessary to be an artist are talent, taste, determination, and generosity. Each of these characteristics are partially innate and partially learned. Talent is specific and recognizable, often at a young age. But it can be developed through training. Taste is inherent. Some prefer sweet and some savory. But taste can also change and develop through exposure. Determination is another nature or nurture phenomenon, but it is necessity for anyone considering being an artist. Finally, generosity. The artist must be willing to release the work. This is not always easy because it is often the best work which is taken. Even if it is sold, there is likely to be more than meets the eye, more than your money's worth, especially on the initial sale. That is because, no matter how thick a skin the artist has developed, there is still a desire for validation, approval, appreciation, which ultimately must include the sale of art.

Mimesis in the Digital Age (2006)

I will begin by laying out a few terms. "Imaging" is the term which has been adapted to denote the use of digital technology to produce images, whether for screen or print. The verb and the gerund forms of the noun "image," was coined in 1992 by Adobe Photoshop, a bitmap graphics editor first trademarked and released in 1990. The digital production and editing of images marks the third age of photography.

To use the term "photography" to apply to the Renaissance may seem anachronistic when that word was coined by Sir John Herschel in a paper read before the Royal Society on March 14, 1839, but I use it nevertheless because in modern parlance it has come to mean any activity which involves the use of a camera. In the 16th century, the camera obscura, literally "dark chamber" (from the Latin) referred to a black box with a lens that could project images of external objects. It was used by painters such as Caravaggio and Vermeer to project images directly onto the canvas from which they could be traced. This controversial theory was first advanced by the artist, David Hockney. His book, Secret Knowledge : Rediscovering the Lost Techniques of the Old Masters, illustrates the contrasting results of two techniques, "eyeballing," as he calls it and lens based composition. The latter, he believes was largely responsible for the realism, and even hyper-realism of many Renaissance paintings.

The early optical instruments or had the ability to project an image but not to fix it. It was in the second era that chemical processes were found that could fix the image. As is the case with many new technologies before standardization, there were many different approaches to the medium including tintypes, ambrotypes (printed on glass plates), and daguerreotypes to name a few. Although prototypes of enlargers were invented early, they weren't widely used until the introduction of high quality small format cameras, such as the Leica, introduced in 1913. Enlarging lent scalability to photography.

There are many points of resemblance between chemical photography and digital imaging, but what is the major difference? A digital image can be sorted by pixels through software applications into a very large number of categories. It can be sorted by contrast, color, shade, area, and many other ways. Any of the resulting sorts can be isolated for a variety of uses or imported into other pictures or even other forms of digitized media without any loss of quality. It is the first time that the reproduction has not deteriorated in relation to the original.

Historically, the reproduction degenerated in quality with each generation. Even with such a comparatively modern medium as film, both motion picture and still, the original negative is maintained from which first generation prints are made. Alfred Stieglitz wrote to his publisher in 1931: "My photographs do not lend themselves to reproduction. The quality of touch in its deepest living sense is inherent in my photographs. When that sense of touch is lost, the heartbeat of the photograph is extinct. In the reproduction, it would become extinct – dead. My interest is in the living. That is why I cannot give permission to reproduce my photographs." (cited from Dorothy Norman's text from *Aperture's History of Photography* series.)

In his seminal essay, "The Work of Art in the Age of Mechanical Reproduction," published in 1936, Walter Benjamin described the inexorable advance of the "exhibition value" as compared to the inherent or "cult value" of art, but the advent of photography accelerated this trend, as he noted in the essay. While the original work, whether painting or theatrical production, makes certain demands, sometimes including a pilgrimage even to see it, the reproduction is ubiquitous, untethered to place.

The popular arts have always existed, but the art and technology of reproduction has brought them to a position of dominance. An article in the New York Times Art & Architecture section (March 30, 1997) entitled "Living With the Fake, and Liking It" by Ada Louise Huxtable, begins: "I do not know just when we lost our sense of reality or our interest in it, but at some point it was decided that reality was not the only option. It was possible, permissible and even desirable to improve on it; one could substitute a more agreeable product. ...Surrogate experience and synthetic settings have become the preferred American way of life." She goes on to document the proliferation of the ersatz or imitative in the most concrete and, if I may coin a word, "non-virtual" of the arts– architecture. "Las Vegas style is in."

The ascent and overwhelming triumph of popular culture encouraged by the development of better and easier means of reproduction has magnified recent history at the expense of the more distant past in nearly every walk of life. Perhaps this leveling of taste is a reaction against the snobbery and preoccupation with the past which characterized the Victorian Age and the Romantics. Or perhaps the rate of change has become so swift that we can now feel nostalgia for the more recent past. Or perhaps the medium of photography tends to encapsulate experience giving us instant nostalgia.

In 2005 I visited a small museum in Gulfport, Mississippi (a year before hurricane Katrina severely damaged it). I had gone to see the work of the regional artist, Walter Anderson, which included a room of a community center in which he had painted the walls, doors, windows, and ceiling. The museum also had an exhibit of photographs by Eudora

Welty before she became a Pulitzer prizewinning author. I had never known her as a photographer. I had studied, in college, the work of the photographers of the Farm Security Administration such as Dorothea Lange, Walker Evans, Russell Lee, and Gordon Parks, but I liked Miss Welty's photographs the best of all. Not only did she have the production values, the sense of composition, the selectivity, the eye for the representative, the sense of composition, but she had something else that the others did not, the sense of belonging, the sense of place. Blacks and whites, these were her neighbors. Yet she said that she gave up photography and took up writing because she believed that she could reveal far more.

Plato denigrated art. Since art imitates physical things, which in turn imitate the Forms, art is always a copy of a copy, mere mimesis, leading us further from truth and toward illusion. But art has never been re-creation; it has always been creation. Its purpose has never been to duplicate but to amaze. It does this not by copying but by altering. Fortunately, Plato also disagreed with himself and presents another view of artist as prophet. As art freed itself from the role of representing nature, photography stepped in as mimesis not only of nature but of art. It works best when it appears not as pastiche but as serendipity, though the post-modernist penchant for bad taste has elevated pastiche, both historical and topical, as in the work of Cindy Sherman.

The march of progress, whether in the sciences or the arts, has been steadily toward the acknowledgment and employment of the counter intuitive. Two examples: contrary to appearances, the sun does not move around the earth; and, contrary to appearances, the columns of the Parthenon were not made perfectly straight or they would not have looked straight. The bulged in the middle in order to correct the optical illusion that a long line that is truly straight will tend to appear to be concave. In addition, all of the columns tip in very slightly. Mimesis is not an exact copy and never was- not until the Digital Age.

92

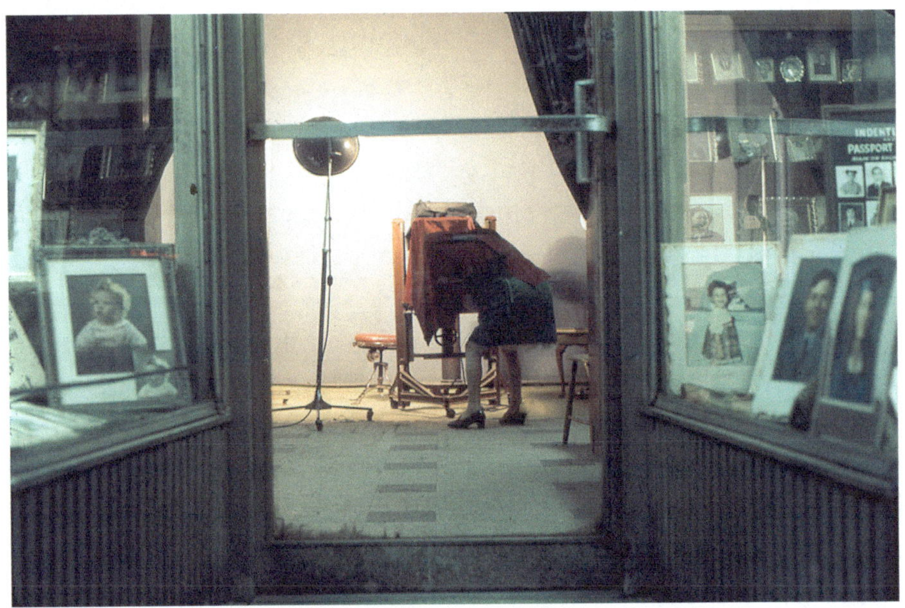

The Photography Studio, New York City (1976)

Monet and Abramović at MOMA (2010)

And they cried aloud, and cut themselves after their manner with knives and lancets, till the blood gushed out upon them.

- I Kings 18:28

Beauty demands to be observed. This is the first principle of aesthetics derived from Greek philosophy. Like many other things, the perception of beauty is partly innate and partly culturally determined. Monet and other impressionists from the Salon des Refusés caused a riot when their paintings were first exhibited. Their paintings were seen as haphazard, lacking form or discipline. And yet Monet's "Water Lilies" are seen today as the epitome of beauty.

What we perceive as beauty is the quality present in a thing or person that gives intense pleasure or deep satisfaction to the mind, whether arising from shape, color, or sound. Although tastes change and different schools of art arise, the goal was still the objectification of beauty. Perhaps art as the pure pursuit and rendering of beauty ended with the death of Monet in 1926.

Until that time, art was concerned with the depiction of beauty and truth, which were seen as Keats depicted them in his "Ode to a Grecian Urn" as equivalent or at least complimentary. This belief may have stemmed from a nearly universal belief in a benevolent order that ultimately rendered truth and beauty compatible. That worldview ended with WWI, the time at which Monet's later paintings turned darker.

Modern art including both non-representational and non-objective art, began more than a decade before Monet's death, but it was still a pursuit of beauty and order, if perhaps a different standard of beauty borrowed from other cultures. It was really not modernism but post-modernism that sought to save art by destroying it, to paraphrase the infamous Vietnam era statement: "We wanted to save the village by destroying it."

The ancient Greek physician Hippocrates coined the phrase: "Life is short; art is long." And since art is long, the effect is cumulative. For example, humanism, the concept that "man is the measure of all things," has remained in the forefront or sometimes in the background. Whether or not a work of art has any other attribute or "higher purpose," it is inherently a celebration of the human spirit, a celebration of life. Post-Modernism attempts to pull down the edifice by chipping away at the foundations. Man is not the measure of all things. Art is temporary. Its purpose is not aesthetic but didactic.

This essay is transcribed from notes I made at two concurrent exhibitions at the Museum of Modern Art in the spring of 2010, Monet's Water Lilies and a retrospective of the performance artist, Marina Abramović including her new performance piece, "The Artist is Present." This work is, in my eyes, a celebration of death. She takes on the role of Medusa (though the allusion is not mentioned) turning her subjects, anyone who looks at her, into stone as she sits motionless for hours, days, weeks, facing a succession of frozen volunteers who return her stare.

Upstairs there are at least a dozen more live victims, mostly undressed, in uninteresting poses. One woman occasionally blinks as she lies under a skeleton. A couple sits back to back with their hair tied together. It seems like torture, like sadomasochism. In a video screen she coolly describes cannibalism in rats; a pile of little bones lies on the gallery floor. And what is sadomasochism without a little sex? Another video shows ululating women running toward the camera and lifting their skirts to reveal their vaginas, while on another screen a field full of naked men hump the ground, butts bobbing up and down. It may be some form of fertility rite, but sterile, banal, robbed of all sensuality, drained of life.

Bit it is not only beauty that demands our attention, so does horror. The word "geek" originally referred to a carnival side-show performer who elicited shock and disgust by biting the head off a live chicken, a performance which always draws a crowd. Such a performance could not carry the warranty that "no animals were harmed in this production."

Performance art, since its inception in the 1960's has often involved self-abuse, self-abasement and even self-inflicted bodily harm. In the performance piece, "Shoot" (1971) by Chris Burden, the artist had a friend shoot him in the arm at a distance of thirteen feet. The plan was for the bullet to graze his arm, but it landed him in the hospital. To add injury to injury, in 1973 he had himself crucified to the roof of a Volkswagen Beetle.

Abramović's first performance was in that same year. It was an extreme version of the game called mumblety peg, or, as it is called in Russia, "Five Finger Fillet," in which she used quick rhythmic knife jabs aimed between her splayed fingers. She titled it "Rhythm 10." After cutting herself twenty times, each time with an increasingly larger blade, she sought to actually replicate her mistakes. Several of her performances since then have also involved some form of self-inflicted harm, such as the time she carved a Yugoslavian red star into her stomach, whipped her back raw and lay on a crucifix made of ice.

Among performance artists, crucifixion is big. Madonna, who brought a performance art sensibility to the performing arts, popularized the incorporation of the crucifix into sado-masochistic chic. The union of sadomasochism and art precedes the Marquis de Sade and possibly ancient Rome. But since art is the harbinger of norms, one questions whether inflicting harm, even self-harm, is acceptable among consenting adults.

Downstairs at MOMA the scene is like the 1960 British horror film, "Village of the Damned" in which children are able to drain the will of those on whom they fix a withering stare. The movie poster read, "Beware the stare that will paralyze the will of the world." For that matter, how is what we are witnessing upstairs different from porno movies in which the naked human form is directed through repetitive action devoid of character or motive? The answer is that at least the horror and porno flicks are without the pretentiousness. However, unlike Five Finger Fillet, this is a harmless staring contest, although, instead of breaking out laughing, several participants were inexplicably reduced to tears.

Six years before Chris Burden had himself shot, Yoko Ono staged a performance at a hall in New York City called "Cut Piece." Dressed in a suit, she sat down on the floor in the middle of the stage on which she had set a pair of shears. Members of the audience then took turns cutting off a piece of her clothing. Although she submitted herself to public exposure, in this case, at least at the start of the performance, the emperor really did have new clothes, as does Abramović in her red evening gown. Yoko Ono's piece had a political aspect, referencing the objectification of women, which, though it hasn't disappeared, was omnipresent in the James Bond days of 1965.

Politics and art have been bedfellows since antiquity, sometimes with elegance and sometimes in an overbearing manner, and sometimes both. For example, the art and literature that came out of Eastern Europe during Marina Abramović's formative years in Tito's Yugoslavia. There was art in service of the state as well as art which was subversive of the political system. It was the latter, which developed under censorship and economic limitations that found a way to get its message out using the tools of art including symbolism, irony, caricature, drama, transposition of time and place, and allegory, to name a few. The difference between the official art and the subversive art was that one was coercive and other engaging.

The epitome of coercive art in the service of political ends is terrorism, which causes the greatest harm to the greatest number of people. 9/11 was made for TV. The instant replay of the first plane hitting the first tower was seen only after maximum viewership was attained for the live telecast of the second plane hitting the second tower. We were literally made to look.

In conclusion, I will once again quote Hippocrates, who also coined the oath of the medical profession: "First, do no harm." Where is the harm or potential harm in many of the performance pieces described in this essay? First of all, there is the harm to the performers, though undertaken willingly as a consenting adults. Flirting with death has been a leitmotif in performance art. To suffer and even to die for Art is a Romantic notion. However, art should (and I hesitate to use the word "should" in discussing art) sharpen the senses, not dull them.

Repeated exposure to violence, both real and enacted, dulls the senses. This is the greater harm. In this age of sensitivity towards all forms of victimization, why is the victimizing of self on the alter of Art exempt from censure. I am not saying censor, whether there be any "redeeming social value" or not. This was once the litmus test for pornography, which, whether sexual, violent, or both, sometimes does not cause excitement but boredom.

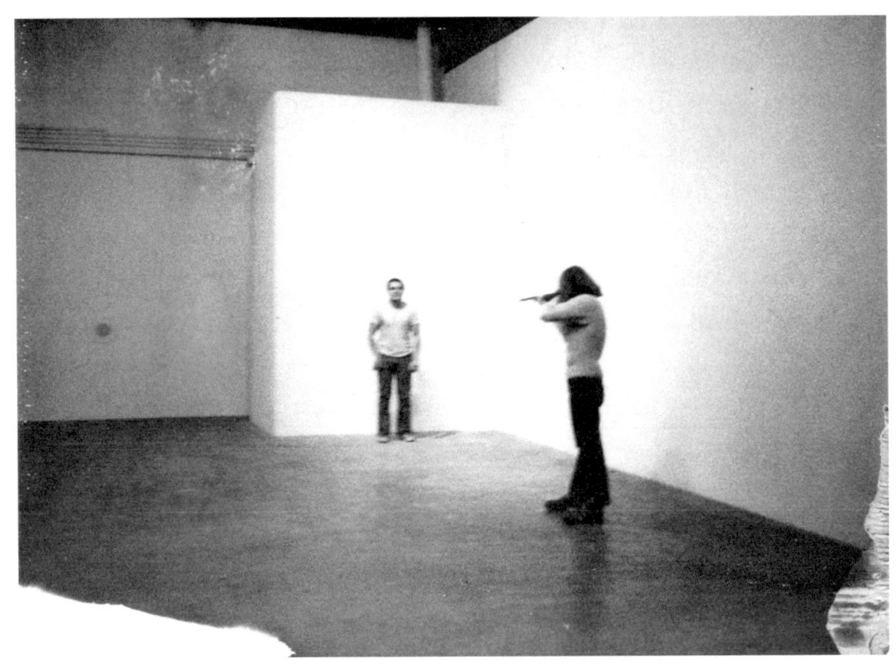

Shoot (1971)

The Nantes School of Architecture and the Idea of Centrality
In hoc signo vinces (2015)

Recently, I toured the campus of the School of Architecture in Nantes with my friend, François, who is on the board of directors. The campus consists of a three story building in a newly restored section of the city on the Loire. The flat roofs of the upper levels are surrounded by parapets, thus adding outdoor working space to the rather spare interior, which resembles a nearly empty warehouse. With the exception of the computer lab which was isolated in a glassed off section, the only object on each floor was a minimalist sculpture. These consisted of sticks or wooden bars in various arrays and stabilized with wire or cable. They had been produced by students based on their research on Buckminster Fuller. "In contrast to the pyramids, columns, and brick-on-brick buildings of the past, which pile solid elements compressively, one on top of the other, Fuller imagined a world full of unconventional structures that maintain their stability, or integrity, through a pervasive tensional force, hence the term (which he coined) *tensegrity.*" (cited from Wikipedia)

It struck me that these sculptures represented the new France. Once a monolithic structure, centralized in King and the Church, or based on the Revolution with its principle of Laïcité, "secularity," France now seeks a new raison d'être to help her to survive and flourish in a post-colonial world. Even though the sculpture may have lacked a single point of centrality, it was held in place by a cable which maintained the tension. The support was in the perimeter, not in the foundation.

"You know," I said, "a major difference between the American and French revolutions is that the American Revolution was not centralized. It consisted of volunteers and conscripts from a loose association of states, whereas the French Revolution was centralized." In fact, the Declaration of Independence never refers to America as a nation, whereas the French Revolution immediately formed a National Assembly. François replied that France has tended toward centralization for more than a thousand years. Since Charlemagne, I added. This centrality has long been the essence of being French.

During the First World War, Edith Wharton wrote a short book, French Ways and Their Meaning, which the U.S. Navy placed aboard all their vessels bound for Europe. The author pointed out that the French have been living on the same land for so long that they know in which cave to age the cheese and which field to plant which grapes to produce various varieties of wine and its distillations. This results in an innate conservatism. If it works so well, why change?

Yet, as with many countries and cultures, there is also a countervailing trend, also pointed out in the book. A tradition of intellectualism has produced an unbroken succession of philosophers from Pascal to Sartre and beyond. For better or worse, Existentialism, Postmodernism, Deconstructionism, Post-structuralism are all French. Since the Revolution, secularism has replaced the Church in most public institutions. However, whether it be the Church, the Revolution, Napoleon, or the string philosophical orthodoxies, the French seem to maintain the positive aspects while forgetting or discarding the many excesses. If the churches and cathedrals have saints and angels whose faces or heads have been knocked off in a moment of zealotry, nobody notices anymore. That too has been assimilated.

The French, like everybody else, are challenged by globalization and it accompanying threats of assimilation and non-assimilation. The American onslaught of mass produced popular culture in the form of movies, music, and other products is perceived as an external threat to the integrity of the French character, and has led at various times to quotas. The Académie Française, official custodian of the French language, actively fights against the incursion of American slang into a language which has gradually been replaced by English for diplomatic intercourse. But, this protective stance has had mixed results, turning cultural imports into forbidden fruits.

The Oxford Dictionary defines integrity as "the state of being whole and undivided." The internal challenge to the integrity of "Frenchness" has been the failure to assimilate millions of immigrants from the former colonies. Integrity entails integration, psychological, cultural, and legal. Part of the failure can be attributed to a disinclination on the part of the immigrants to adopt the French model, first promulgated in the Revolution and renewed under the Napoleonic Code. An important feature of this model is the separation of Church and State, which fosters not only liberty, but also equality and fraternity.

Despite being a nation with deep historical roots and a strong ethnic identity, France has been generally hospitable to her minorities, with some notable exceptions. On August 24, 1572, St. Bartholomew's Day, the queen, Catherine de Medici instigated the slaughter of 70,000 Huguenots, French Protestants. At the end of the 19th century the Dreyfus Affair revealed a deep strain of anti-Semitism which led a young newsman, Theodore Herzl, to envision a solution for the Jews in a Zionist State. Forty years later, the French Vichy Government collaborated with the Nazis and had the French police round up thousands of Jews to be deported to the death camps. Still, unlike most other European countries, 75% of French Jews, with the help of the French, survived in France and her colonies. Like most countries, France has a mixed record.

At the Treaty of Versailles, France had a large role in redrawing the globe upon the collapse of all of the empires after WWI. Austrian, German, Russian, and Ottoman empires and their rulers claimed their legitimacy from God. Even Great Britain lost her empire not long afterwards. It was France that led the way to the post-imperial, post divinely constituted, secular Europe, something for which the Vatican took a long time to forgive her.

However, the question remains: can these sticks form a stable structure without a point of centrality. This is the challenge of Post-Christian Europe which once marched all the way to Jerusalem behind only two perpendicular sticks joined together at the center. If, on the other hand, equilibrium can be maintained with a more complex arrangement with multiple stress points and more than one core, which is the Post-Modern view, then only time will test its stability.

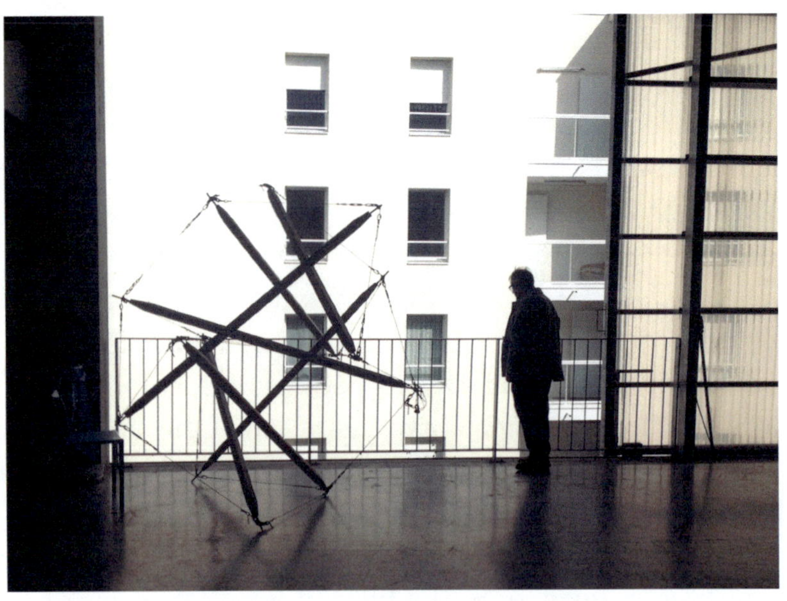

François at the School of Architecture

The Evolution of Propaganda (2017)

The apocalypse has become a cliché. According to the metrics of its usage in published books as compiled by statisticians who measure such things, its nadir was reached in 1939 and since then its use has doubled. One might think this would be a result of an increase in millennialism ("the end is near") such as what gave rise to the Crusades a thousand years ago. However, I am convinced that the word, stemming from the Greek for "revelation," a name which it shares as the title of the last book of the New Testament, is often used today in a metaphorical sense to depict any catastrophe, past or impending. For example, global warming might be described as an environmental apocalypse.

Meanwhile, the use of the word "propaganda" has declined by two-thirds since its peak in 1945. I was born shortly after this and began to study it in my senior year of high school in an advanced placement class generically called "Seminar." We learned, in broad strokes, how propaganda uses linkage to mold opinions. For example, advertisers might link their products to motherhood or the national flag. We learned that the word "propaganda" stems from Congregatio de Propaganda Fide, the Office for the Propagation of the Faith, which was established by the Catholic Church in the 1600's to train priests for missions and to counter the Reformation. I was in high school when I read two complimentary versions of a dystopian future, 1984 and Brave New World. In 1984, Winston Smith works as a clerk in the Records Department of the Ministry of Truth, where his job is to rewrite historical documents so they match the constantly changing party line.

At the university I majored in Radio, TV, and Film. The head of the department, Dr. Jack Ellis, was a pioneer in the study of film as a serious art form. His bibliography of published books traces his focus from film history in general to the documentary film and finally to the uses of film as propaganda. We studied the films, the techniques, and even the experiments of Sergei Eisenstein, the Soviet silent film director who contributed much to the theory and practice of "montage" or inter-cutting to create an emotional response.

The "Kuleshov effect" had been first demonstrated by Soviet filmmaker Lev Kuleshov in the 1910s and 1920s. It is a mental phenomenon by which viewers derive more meaning from the interaction of two sequential shots than from a single shot in isolation. Kuleshov edited a short film in which a shot of the expressionless face of Tsarist matinee idol, Ivan Mosjoukine, was alternated with various other shots (a plate of soup, a girl in a coffin, a woman on a divan). The film was shown to an audience who believed that the expression on Mosjoukine's face was different each time he appeared, depending on whether he was "looking at" the plate of soup, the girl in the coffin, or the woman on the divan, showing an expression of hunger, grief or desire, respectively. The footage of Mosjoukine was actually the same shot each time. According to one report, the audience raved over the actor's skill in depicting these various moods.

The next step in the evolution of propaganda is when the tail began to wag the dog. By the time of Hitler's rise to power, film had become a highly developed craft with major contributions from German directors such as Fritz Lang, famous for his use of expressionistic camera angles in such films as "The Cabinet of Dr. Caligari," and Ernst Lubitsch, famous for his innovative use of lighting. The Nazi filmmaker, Leni Riefenstahl, utilized a low camera angle to add a heroic stature to Adolph Hitler in her film of the Nuremberg Rally of 1934, "Triumph of the Will". She also created the columns of light, spotlights aimed at the night sky, specifically for the film though this effect undoubtedly also inspired the actual attendees of the rally. Thirty cameras were in operation making a case that the entire rally was staged for the film. Propaganda was such an important function in the Nazi government that its minister, Hermann Göring, was second in command to Hitler. Perhaps that is why the usage of the word "propaganda" reached its peak in 1945.

In the post-war era, many of the techniques of propaganda were utilized by the advertising industry. The Hidden Persuaders by Vance Packard was published in 1957 in which eight basic human needs are identified which advertisers try to address. They are: emotional security; reassurance of worth; ego gratification; creative outlets; love objects; sense of power; roots; and immortality. In such a list as this, they all seem to blend together, but each is addressed individually. Packard also discussed the dangers of subliminal advertising, which was banned in Britain and the United States, though its use and efficacy was only a rumor, probably exacerbated by the brainwashing scare arising out of the Korean War.

More than twenty years ago, my sister-in-law forwarded a fascinating article about how freedom produces surprising results. It began with the observation that capitalism, which envisioned economic freedom from the feudalism that had existed in Europe, was expected to produce in America a society of independent craftsmen and farmers. In other words, production would be decentralized with each producer sending his goods to a central market or fair. Instead, with industrialization production became centralized in factories and industrialized farms ,and at the same time, distribution became decentralized. Montgomery Ward produced the first mail order catalog in America in 1872. Before long, Sears and J.C. Penney were sending their catalogs to homes in every farm and factory town across the land. At the same time, advertisers were reaching out to a broad audience through the developing mass-media. Mass marketing techniques found their way into many realms including politics and religion.

Many experts believe that in the first televised presidential debate, in 1960, Nixon won on the radio while Kennedy won on T.V. The entire debate lasted one hour. A hundred years earlier, in the Lincoln-Douglas debates, of which there were seven, whoever spoke first would open with an hour long address. The other would then speak for an hour and a half. The first then had 30 minutes of rebuttal. This format appealed to a more literary sensibility which allowed a deep analytic, even philosophical approach to the issues, the main one at the time being slavery.

More than 150 years later, the issue still is slavery – not the literal owning of human beings as chattel to be exploited in involuntary servitude, but rather the right to privacy of the individual's thoughts. This is the main area that is attacked and colonized in the two dystopian novels previously mentioned. But this conquest of the human mind and will can occur in different ways.

In 1949, Aldous Huxley, author of *Brave New World*, wrote a letter to George Orwell upon the publication of *1984*:

Wrightwood. Cal.
21 October, 1949

Dear Mr. Orwell,

It was very kind of you to tell your publishers to send me a copy of your book. It arrived as I was in the midst of a piece of work that required much reading and consulting of references; and since poor sight makes it necessary for me to ration my reading, I had to wait a long time before being able to embark on Nineteen Eighty-Four.

Agreeing with all that the critics have written of it, I need not tell you, yet once more, how fine and how profoundly important the book is. May I speak instead of the thing with which the book deals --- the ultimate revolution? The first hints of a philosophy of the ultimate revolution --- the revolution which lies beyond politics and economics, and which aims at total subversion of the individual's psychology and physiology --- are to be found in the Marquis de Sade, who regarded himself as the continuator, the consummator, of Robespierre and Babeuf. The philosophy of the ruling minority in Nineteen Eighty-Four is a sadism which has been carried to its logical conclusion by going beyond sex and denying it. Whether in actual fact the policy of the boot-on-the-face can go on indefinitely seems doubtful. My own belief is that the ruling oligarchy will find less arduous and wasteful ways of governing and of satisfying its lust for power, and these ways will resemble those which I described in Brave New World. I have had occasion recently to look into the history of animal magnetism and hypnotism, and have been greatly struck by the way in which, for a hundred and fifty years, the world has refused to take serious cognizance of the discoveries of Mesmer, Braid, Esdaile, and the rest.

Partly because of the prevailing materialism and partly because of prevailing respectability, nineteenth-century philosophers and men of science were not willing to investigate the odder facts of psychology for practical men, such as politicians, soldiers and policemen, to apply in the field of government. Thanks to the voluntary ignorance of our fathers, the advent of the ultimate revolution was delayed for five or six generations. Another lucky accident was Freud's inability to hypnotize successfully and his consequent disparagement of hypnotism. This delayed the general application of hypnotism to psychiatry for at least forty years. But now psycho-analysis is being combined with hypnosis; and hypnosis has been made easy and indefinitely extensible through the use of barbiturates, which induce a hypnoid and suggestible state in even the most recalcitrant subjects.

Within the next generation I believe that the world's rulers will discover that infant conditioning and narco-hypnosis are more efficient, as instruments of government, than clubs and prisons, and that the lust for power can be just as completely satisfied by suggesting people into loving their servitude as by flogging and kicking them into obedience. In other words, I feel that the nightmare of Nineteen Eighty-Four is destined to modulate into the nightmare of a world having more resemblance to that which I imagined in Brave New World. The change will be brought about as a result of a felt need for increased efficiency. Meanwhile, of course, there may be a large-scale biological and atomic war --- in which case we shall have nightmares of other and scarcely imaginable kinds.

Thank you once again for the book.

Yours sincerely,
Aldous Huxley

In short, Huxley believed it more likely that the human will could be subverted, not through coercion but voluntarily, through a combination of factors related to sado-masochism, hypnotism, addiction and entertainment. Though I have not consigned 1984 to the fires of that other dystopia described in Ray Bradbury's Farenheit 451, I favor Huxley's vision as the more prescient. Each of these novels describes repression in its various forms, and each has had its antecedents in Nazism, in Stalinism, in the Inquisition, to name a few. In terms of the present, I believe a Brave New World is the bigger risk. On the other hand, perhaps that only holds for the Western world. In the Middle East, for example, there are modesty patrols enforcing female attire, endemic torture, ubiquitous secret police and heavy handed propaganda, all more reminiscent of 1984. I am a dual citizen residing both in the uttermost West and the Middle East, but since my subject is the evolution of propaganda, I believe that the innovations in propaganda have been far greater in the Western World.

But before I leave the Middle East, however, I would like to further illuminate this contrast in the techniques of brainwashing and propaganda between the East and the West with the history of a sect called the Assassins. The origins of the Assassins can be traced back to just before the First Crusade, around 1080 in Persia. Hassan-i Sabbah founded the cult whether for personal power or in reaction to internecine strife within the Muslim world, or due to the incursion of Crusaders in the Holy Land, or for all of these factors combined. The one motivation that is certain is that Sabbah wanted to establish what he called an Islamic State, or specifically, as he referred to it by the name of his sect, a Nizari Ismaili state. He searched for a location that would be fit for a headquarters and decided on the fortress at Alamut in what is now northwestern Iran. He adapted the fortress to suit his needs not only for defense from hostile forces, but also for indoctrination of his followers. He then began expanding his influence outwards to nearby towns and districts, using his agents to gain political favor and to intimidate the local populations.

Below Sabbah, the Grand Headmaster of the Order, were those known as "Greater Propagandists", followed by the normal "Propagandists", the Rafiqs ("Companions"), and the Lasiqs ("Adherents"). It was the Lasiqs who were trained to become some of the most feared assassins, or as they were called, "Fida'i" (self-sacrificing agent), in the known world. The disciples who carried out these suicide missions were generally intelligent and well-read because they were required to possess not only knowledge about their enemy, but his or her culture and native language. They were trained by their masters to disguise themselves and sneak into enemy territory to perform the assassinations, instead of simply attacking their target outright.

One hundred and fifty years later Marco Polo recounted a story he had heard during his travels to the Orient, of the "Old Man of the Mountain" who would drug his young followers with hashish, lead them to a "paradise", and then claim that only he had the means to allow for their return. Perceiving that Sabbah was either a prophet or magician, his disciples, believing that only he could return them to "paradise", were fully committed to his cause and willing to carry out his every request. Hence the term "assassin" - from hashish. Others dispute this etymology, writing that Hassan Sabbah called his disciples Asasiyun, meaning people who are faithful to the Asās, meaning "foundation" of the faith. Whatever the case semantically, whether the inspiration was the promise of seventy virgins or the propagation of the faith, this story illustrates that in a thousand years, from the cult of assassins to the cult of ISIS, nothing has changed. Of course, to apply the term "propagandist" to 11th century Persia is anachronistic, but the principle remains. Terrorism is psychological warfare with most of the intended effect being disseminated by the media, fully understanding the newsroom axiom, "If it bleeds it leads."

Now let's take a look at the alternate method of producing conditioned responses through positive reinforcement, through the activation of our dopamine receptors. We are talking about fine tuning here. Chocalatiers, casinos, and drug pushers have long been involved in triggering the release of dopamine in the brain. To some extent they have each set up shop in what they believe is the most profitable locations. But "big data" can now be mined not according to one's zip code, nor according to one's affiliations, but individually, based strictly on one's non-private postings and "likes" on Facebook, one's choices and ratings of movies on Netflix or music on Pandora. The use of big data has been used recently to produce surprising wins in two recent political campaigns, Brexit and Trump. In fact, Trump's chief adviser is on the board of directors of one of the pioneering firms in mining and utilizing big data, Cambridge Analytica. It is uncertain how big a factor this was, but it is possible that the recent campaign was, among other things, a contest between big data and advanced "psychographics" versus mere demographics. Messages do not need to be consistent, only targeted and on point. Things usually proceed in small increments until they reach a breaking point, somewhat like plate tectonics shift constantly giving rise to small earthquakes that mostly go unnoticed. Knowing whether we are at the breaking point is as difficult as predicting an earthquake. In other words, the apocalypse is always late, until it happens.

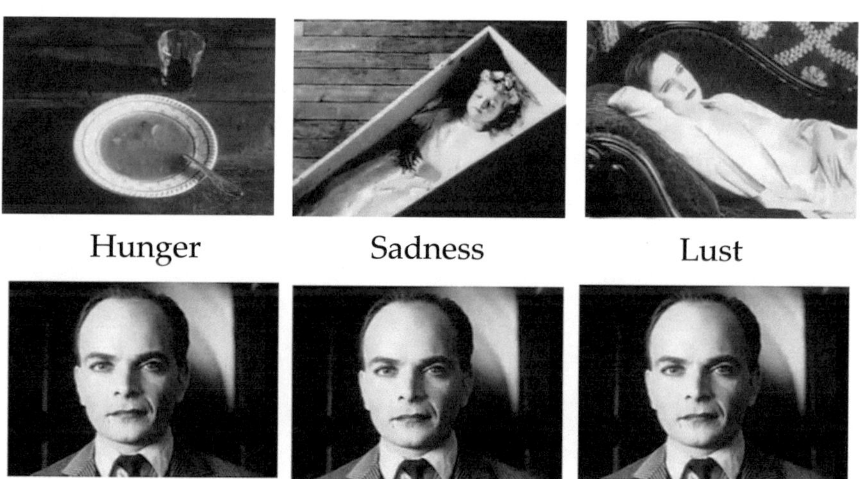

<table>
<tr><td>Hunger</td><td>Sadness</td><td>Lust</td></tr>
</table>

Stills from Kuleshov's Experiment

Afterword

Unlike the expressionless face on the previous page, the faces carved in the choir stalls at Winchester Cathedral bear many expressions. This is the face of the public, with all of its foibles, circa 1300. The cathedral was the public works program of its time and place. This was possible because England at the time had become a fairly homogeneous society. The Vikings and all other invaders had been assimilated, the Jews had been expelled, and the Reformation had not yet taken place. The town was the parish as they attempted to build a perfect society.

America, on the other hand, was founded on the principle of privacy – private property and privacy of conscience in a heterodox and polyglot society. The question is, what is the glue that will hold it together? Roads, sewers, and a legal system, like the Roman Empire? Art and commerce, like the Florentine Republic? Both exercised military force, often hired. An all volunteer army, some believe, is one of the hallmarks of empire. Perhaps it is a dynamic balance between the private and the public, between the particular and the universal, that maintains the health of a society.

And what is the role of the artist? Recluse or celebrity, prophet or clown, critic or celebrant. Plato, while advocating for a philosopher king, sought to censor both art and music. Since the arts shape the character, he thought, they must be strictly controlled in order to create an ideal society. Beware utopians and idealogues, or, to paraphrase Voltaire, "the perfect is the enemy of the good.

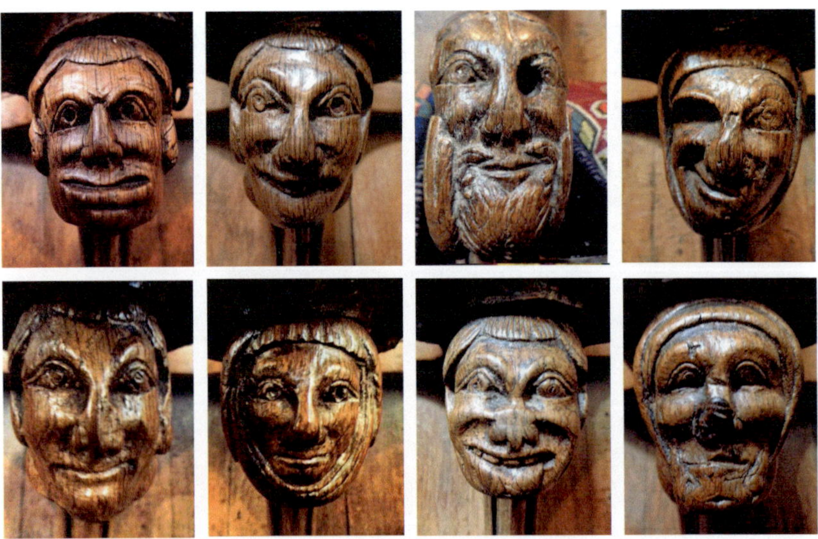

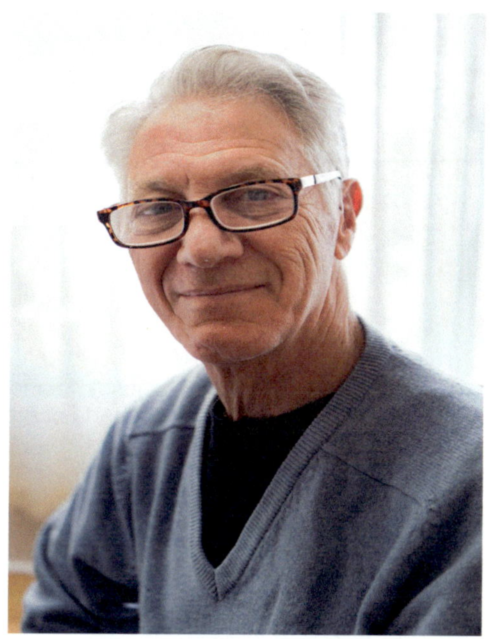

Photo: Judith Fern Productions

Chaim Bezalel was born in 1949 in New York City. He is a graduate of Northwestern University, where he majored in Radio, TV, and Film. He and his wife, Yonnah Ben Levy, with whom he often collaborates, live in Stanwood, WA and Ashkelon, Israel. In addition to painting and sculpture and photography, he is also a published poet, musician, and songwriter.

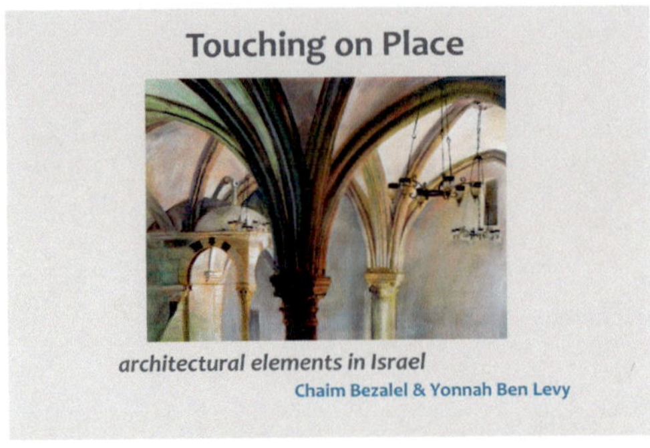

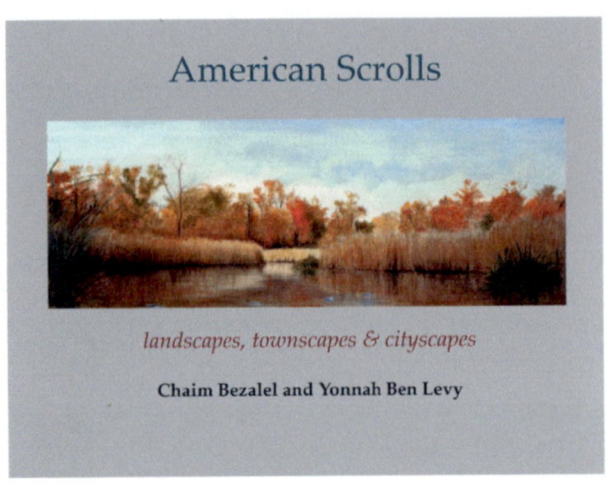

ISBN 978-0-9995958-0-0, 87 p. 6 x 9 in.
77 original paintings plus photographs done over twenty-five years convey the history of the past two millennia in this historic land. The book is arranged geographically with a brief account of each region and site. $20

ISBN 978-0-9995958-4-8,120 p. 8 ½ x 11
134 mostly panoramic paintings from different parts of America including Autumn Scrolls, Pacific Scrolls, Gulf Scrolls, Desert Scrolls, and Community. Many of these paintings are now in public collections. $30

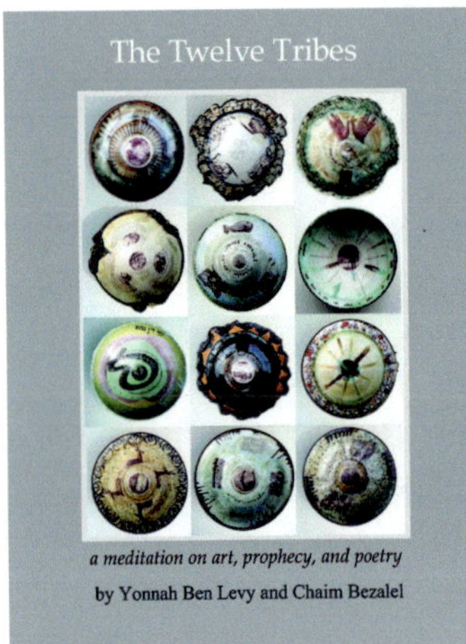

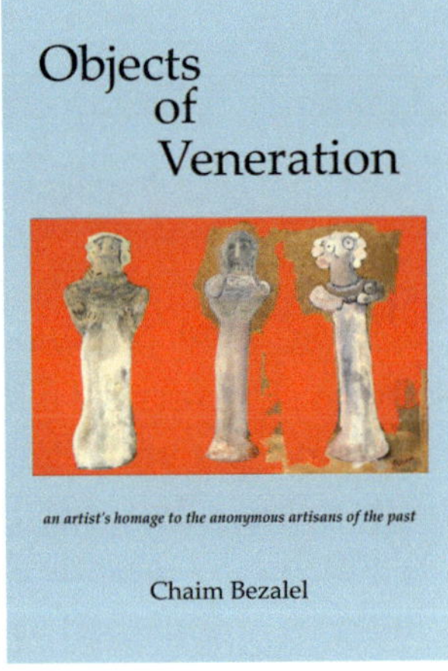

ISBN 978-0-9995958-3-1
54 p. 8 ½ x 11 in.
Two different but related art collaborations, "Bowls of Blessing" (2011) and "Urim & Thummim"(1991), Meditations on the meaning and role of Israel in history and oracle. $20

ISBN 978-0-9995958-1-7
86 p. 9 x 6 in.
Paintings and sculpture inspired by devotional objects from around the world in the artist's or in other private and public collections. Includes a 33 page essay, "The Talmud,a Brief Travelogue." $20

ISBN 978-0-9995958-5-5
120 p. 9 x 6 in.
A 38 year old ex-hippie, ex-stockbroker on the lam boards a plane to Israel, where he has never been, with a one way ticket and two suitcases. Two years later, he is drafted into the Israeli army reserves. This is his journal. $15

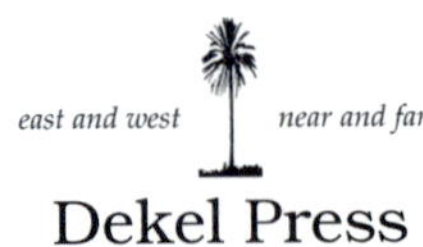

For information or orders please visit our website:
www.dekelpress.com

Made in the USA
Monee, IL
07 July 2026

56549089R00071